WAITING FOR
PETE
TO GO HOME

DONNA MANDER-FISER

TATE PUBLISHING & *Enterprises*

Published by Tate Publishing & Enterprises, LLC
127 E. Trade Center Terrace | Mustang, Oklahoma 73064 USA
1.888.361.9473 | www.tatepublishing.com

Tate Publishing is committed to excellence in the publishing industry. The company reflects the philosophy established by the founders, based on Psalm 68:11,
"The Lord gave the word and great was the company of those who published it."

Book design copyright © 2010 by Tate Publishing, LLC. All rights reserved.
Cover design by Kristen Verser
Interior design by Stefanie Rane

Published in the United States of America

ISBN: 978-1-61739-640-3
1. Biography & Autobiography, Personal Memoirs
2. Biography & Autobiography, Medical
10.10.25

DEDICATION

Waiting for Pete to Go Home is dedicated with eternal love to the memory of my husband, Peter John Mander.

WAITING FOR
PETE
TO GO HOME

Acknowledgements

I could never have written this story if not for my mom. She believed in me and everything I did. Even though she wasn't with me physically during the time I wrote my story, I always felt her presence. She was always at my shoulder telling me I could do it. My mom would be so proud!

I will forever be grateful to our sons, Matthew and Mark. Throughout those long eighteen months, they carried me while I carried them. Their love and support was endless.

I wish to thank my sisters, Hope and Ruthie, my brother Philip, my brother and sister-in-law, Dick and Cyndi, our friends Geri and Gene and Barb and Joel for their continuous support and encouragement during Pete's illness. Their love of Pete was clearly shown through their dedication to him.

Most of all, I thank God. All credit goes to him.

TABLE OF
CONTENTS

INTRODUCTION

My story is about love. It is about the love between a man and a woman that is promised when wedding vows are spoken—for better or for worse, in sickness and in health. My husband, Pete, and I were married almost thirty-eight years. We had many, many years of health and happiness with only a few bumps along the way, but in December of 2000, Pete was diagnosed with brain cancer. This is my story about all the years of happiness and joy we had before sickness and death came into our life, and subsequently, how we dealt with Pete's illness and dying. Your story may be different from mine; however, in sharing my story, my prayer is that it will bring hope and comfort to those who read it. I write this story and share it with you because I want others to know that they are not alone, their feelings are not wrong, there is always room for hope, and sometimes, just sometimes, you get another chance at happiness. Here is my story.

First Meeting

The first time I saw Pete, I thought he looked like a total fool. I was only seventeen years old, out of high school, and working at my first job in Springfield, Illinois. Pete was a twenty-year-old college student. We were both at the same house party. I arrived at the party much later than Pete. This, I could tell by his behavior. As I entered the room, the music was so loud it was bouncing off the walls and the smell of beer saturated the air. Everyone seemed to be with a partner and I felt a little alone and lost. This didn't seem to be the case with Pete. One of the first things I saw was this obnoxious, short guy dancing with a big bosomed gal. This guy, I thought, looked pretty stupid because he was thrashing about without any rhythm. Instead of moving with the music, he used only his feet, and in such a way that he kept traveling backwards. It was obvious that he thought he was pretty cool. He was a total turn-off for me. But, little did I know that in a few short months, this show-offy little guy and I would fall in love. Pete would become my world.

A few weeks after first seeing Pete, I saw him at a local hangout. I remember standing across the room from him and each time I looked his way, he was looking at me. He finally came over to me and started a conversation. I found him to be different from my first impression. He wasn't the arrogant person that I first thought. Actually he seemed a little unsure of himself. We became acquainted during that conversation and found that we actually had some of the same values and goals. I could tell that he was someone that I wanted to know much better. Thus, began our dating.

DATING BEGINS

Since Pete was a college student without much money, our dating pretty much consisted of staying home. I had a rental apartment I shared with three roommates and that is where Pete and I spent our time. We would buy a couple of pot pies and spend the evening in front of the television. After we were married and wanted to reminisce our dating days, we would have pot pies. As silly as it sounds, pot pies brought warmth into our relationship. It made us remember the days of falling in love.

On one of our first dates, we were driving along Fifth Street in Springfield during a bad snow storm. When we came to the intersection, four of the five lanes had stalled, abandoned cars blocking their lane. We drove up to the only open lane and immediately got stuck. Just about that time, we heard a siren. When we looked behind us, an ambulance was coming with lights flashing. There was no way the ambulance could get through. Pete panicked, got out of the car, and tried pushing his car by himself. He made no headway at all. After a few minutes of waiting, the ambulance was able to turn around and take a different route. I remember that night so vividly. Even though I could see the funny side of the situation with Pete trying to push the car by himself, I also saw a man who saw a serious situation and took the responsibility of trying to correct it. That was my Pete, Mr. Responsibility!

One evening, our date involved sitting on a country road counting cars. The company Pete worked for needed to determine how many cars traveled that particular road. You can imagine how boring and lonely that could be, so I went with him. We were there for hours and counted only a few cars. Of course, most of the time we were so busy making out that we didn't even notice the cars. The company determined, through Pete's report, that there wasn't enough traffic on that road to warrant keeping it open. The accuracy of that report is still in question.

House parties were popular in those days, so if we did go out, we would usually end up at someone's apartment or maybe their home if their parents were out of town. We most often met up with a large group of friends. Pete had several buddies that he said were always hitting on women. It didn't take him long to let them know that I was off limits to them. I belonged to Pete.

A DIAMOND RING

We had been dating about six months when, one evening, Pete gave me an engagement ring. I cried when he gave it to me, not out of happiness or surprise, but because I could not see how it would work out. Pete was Catholic and I was Baptist. My parents did not like the Catholic religion and his parents only liked the Catholic religion. I cannot tell you the number of times I heard my dad say, "Those Catholics go out and drink and smoke on Saturday night and then go to church on Sunday and the priest forgives them." I grew up with this type of prejudice. I knew marrying a Catholic would cause great distress for my dad.

Even though my family had already met Pete, the night we went to see them to tell them we were engaged was pretty scary for both of us. Dad immediately puffed up and said he wouldn't walk me down the aisle. He said I should not be marrying a Catholic. He said to me, "Do you know that you are going to have to sign papers to say that your kids will be Catholic?" He was really in a stew. My oldest brother, Phil, was there and spoke up and said he would walk me down the aisle. Dad settled down a little then and conceded that if we waited one year before getting married, he would walk me down the aisle. We ended up waiting about eighteen months before marrying.

Vows Spoken

Pete and I were married June 6, 1964. We were married in St. Joseph's Catholic Church in Springfield, Illinois. My dad did walk me down the aisle. I was nineteen and Pete was twenty-two. As I look back, we were just a couple of kids who saw only the good in life.

Our reception was held in my hometown of Mt. Olive, Illinois, which was sixty miles south of Springfield. My parents insisted on having it there; I believe it was their way of having some control. We honeymooned in St. Louis, Missouri. I remember the first night so well. After the lights were off and we were ready for sleep, I felt tears running down my face. I knew this new life of ours was forever.

NEW LIFE/NEW CITY

We started our married life in Rock Island, Illinois. We moved away from all our friends and family to an unknown community. We didn't know a soul. For me, the move away from everyone and everything I was familiar with was traumatic; however, Pete took it in stride. Pete was such a strong person; he never showed apprehension about anything. He knew he was going to be successful and he knew he could take care of me. Pete was offered a job at the Rock Island Arsenal and I received a job offer with Deere & Company in Moline, Illinois. We lived in a small rental apartment with dreams of someday building a home. It didn't take long for us to become friends with several people through our jobs.

A few months after I started work, a few new girlfriends and I joined a bowling league. Pete immediately went out and bought me a red bowling ball with my name on it. He was happy that I had found friends and was adapting to our new life. Since I was uneasy about getting home in the dark and walking from the car to the house, Pete would wait at the window and watch for me. When I drove up, I waited in the car until he came out to get me. He said he didn't want the boogey man to get me. Pete always thought about my happiness and my needs. He would make any sacrifice necessary to make me happy.

BIRTH AND DEATH OF JEFFREY JOHN MANDER

I became pregnant and we had a son on August 16, 1966. We named him Jeffrey John Mander; John was Pete's middle name. It would be hard to find a more proud father than Pete. He strutted around like he was the only man in the world to father a son.

After Jeff was born and I was settled in my room, the nurse brought our son for Pete and me to hold. I don't believe there is anything more precious than holding your first born child. We marveled at our creation. Pete and I just stared at him, touched him, kissed him, and took in the sight of him. We tried to figure out who he looked like, and decided that he really looked like Jeffrey John Mander.

On the day after Jeff was born, Pete was supposed to come to the hospital around 1:00 p.m. He didn't arrive until about 1:30 p.m. When he finally got to my room, he came in sweating profusely, disheveled, and out of breath. He proceeded to tell me that he had locked the car keys in the apartment and had to walk to the hospital. We lived about two miles from the hospital. Now we are talking August, the hottest summer I have ever experienced. Pete could have found help to get into the apartment to get the car keys and then drive to the hospital, but that wasn't him. He knew he should be there for me and nothing else mattered. I laughed and thought it was funny; Pete did not share my humor. We did, however, share that story many times over the years. We loved to share stories.

As I was lying in my bed the next day at the hospital, I saw the nurses bustling around and glancing my way. I immediately felt something was wrong. It could not have been more than half an hour when Pete walked into my room with a somber look. A nurse had called Pete to come to the hospital to talk with the pediatrician. The doctor explained to us that Jeff had become extremely ill and probably would not live. The doctor said that Jeff's heart had not formed right during pregnancy. Jeffrey John Mander died that afternoon. He was only two days old. Pete and I were devastated. We didn't even have time to comprehend what had happened before hospital personnel came to my room and asked permission to do an autopsy on our baby. It was presented to us that we could be saving other children. What do you say when you have been told that your actions are going to save other children? We said "yes." I have always felt if we had been given more time to think, we might not have given permission for an autopsy. Jeffrey John was our creation, and we didn't want a doctor violating his precious little body.

After our son was buried and I came home from the hospital, Pete went back to work and because I had quit my job, I stayed home. Our plan had been that I would not work, but stay home with our baby. You read about couples who lose a child and then have trouble with their own relationship. Actually, that could have happened to us. Pete was back to his normal routine and I was left alone. I didn't feel like he was grieving like I was and I resented it. I don't know why, but Pete and I never talked about Jeff; somehow, we couldn't and I didn't question it. He had his grief and I had mine. You would think that a situation like that would have damaged our relationship, but it didn't. I can't explain to you why we kept our grief to ourselves; I just know that we did. I didn't understand it then and I still do not understand it now. All I know is that we were able to go forward in our relationship without any damage being done. We immediately focused on having another baby.

TRYING AGAIN

I went back to work in a few months and settled into my new job. We were advised to wait at least six months before getting pregnant, but we were anxious to start our family so we waited only three. We were sure I would become pregnant quickly, but it did not happen. Each month that I had not conceived, we would become depressed. We both went to our respective doctors and found that I probably would not conceive again. Jeffrey John Mander was our miracle from God.

We did not let the doctor's opinion deter us from having a family. We decided to adopt. After the preliminary paperwork, a caseworker came for a home visit. During our interview, we told her that we would love to have twins. She told us that it probably would not happen, as there had never been twins in the history of the agency.

ADOPTION OF
MATTHEW AND MARK

In February, 1968, while I was at work, I received a phone call from the caseworker. She told me they had twin boys for us. She added that they were of Polish descent. She told me that one twin could come home with us in a few days, but the second one would have to stay in the hospital longer because he was so small. I called Pete at work and said, "They have twin boys for us and they are Polish." By the time I got home from work that evening, my face physically hurt from smiling. And Pete, well, he was walking on air. We had prayed and prayed for a baby, and not one child did God give us, but two. We immediately started setting up the nursery.

On February 29, 1968, we drove to Peoria to pick up our son. We decided to name him Matthew Martin Mander. It was a beautiful, glorious day. The sun was shining, the weather was warm, and we were bringing our baby home. On April 5, 1968, we made a second trip to Peoria to pick up Mark Andrew Mander. We had both our babies home. Life was good. We had each other and now we had children. We were a real family. We loved our babies and each other so much.

PARENTING

Our babies were our life. We were so proud to have twins. The first couple of months we enjoyed being at home with them. But here we had been blessed with twins, and we wanted to show them off. So one evening, we decided to venture out with the babies. With Pete and I each toting a baby in a carrier, we went to a fast food restaurant. The babies immediately became fussy, so in addition to trying to balance our food tray, we each had to tend to a fussy baby. It turned out to be a very hectic evening for us. The babies were fussy and people were stopping by to see the twins, and plain enough, it just didn't go smoothly. By the end of the evening, we were a little harried and decided maybe we should wait awhile before we went out to eat with the babies again.

When the boys were seven months old, we took them to a photographer to get their picture taken. That was a fun experience because the boys were in great moods. They hammed it up for the photographer and had great pictures taken. When we got home, the boys' continued to have a fun time by chasing each other down the hallway. I can still hear them giggling and see them chasing each other. It was one of those evenings when everything seemed perfect in our world.

We bought hobby horses for both boys. Their ponies provided them hours of entertainment. Each night before going to bed, the ritual was for the boys to take one last ride on their ponies, tell the ponies good night, and give them a kiss. Each morning when the boys woke up, the first thing they did was wake their ponies with a kiss.

When the boys were about two years old, they would ask their dad to tell them a story each night before we put them to bed. Pete could make up the best stories for them. It would almost always be about a troll who lived down the road under the bridge. It was an ongoing story about the troll and two little boys who walked across the bridge. The two little boys, of course, were named Matthew and Mark. The troll and the boys became friends and played together. Pete would never make it a scary story, just fascinating for two little boys who hung on to his every word. I so wish I would have recorded Pete telling his stories. What a precious gift that would make for our grandchildren.

When our boys were about five years old, Mark asked, "Mom, since we have Mother's Day and Father's Day, why don't we have Son's Day?" It sounded reasonable to Pete and me, so we started having Son's Day once a year. We would pick a Sunday in June or

July. Pete painted a big sign for the yard proclaiming "Son's Day." The boys never knew when we were having their special day; it was always a surprise. We would wake them up, take them to the back yard, and there would be the sign and their present. Matthew and Mark loved it until they got a little older and didn't want the whole neighborhood seeing the sign.

One year, we bought them blow-up boats. We had a stream just a little ways down the road from our house. The four of us would carry those boats to the stream and Pete and I would each take one boy and paddle along the stream. Sometimes the water was so shallow we would hit bottom. We would have to get out and move the boat to continue. The boats would snag on debris and get holes and we would find ourselves sitting in water, but we had fun while it lasted.

Another year, the boys received a small tent. That was exciting, as the four of us had to sleep in that tent. It was a little crowded, but we made it through the night. We all four were exhausted and crabby the next day.

One summer, the boys decided they would like a tree house. We did not have a tree in which to build a tree house, so Pete built one on very tall posts. He built it under a weeping willow tree so it had the appearance of a tree house. The boys loved that tree house. They were the only kids in the neighborhood with one, so they had a lot of company. They even had a tree house sale and sold their toys. That was when garage sales had first started, but a tree house sale? The newspaper came out and took a picture of them.

Pete and I loved being parents. We were very protective, almost to the point of being over protective. We wanted to be where our boys were, so we volunteered for every activity they were in. Room mother, Cub Scouts, baseball coach, basketball coach, field trips, PTA—whatever involved Matt and Mark, involved us. The summers of baseball were such happy times for all of us. Pete was the coach, the boys played, and I was their cheerleader. We lived for the baseball games. I'll have to admit that sometimes the boys would rather have had a different coach. Pete was a tough coach; he expected only the best out of each of his players.

We became runners. All four of us would compete in races. Not that we were that good, but it was a good family activity for us. Then, of course, we would all have matching T-shirts.

Pete always had goals for himself and others, so he decided to run a marathon. Matt was sixteen that year and decided to run it with him. They trained for several months. Their long runs would be on Sundays. Pete would come home exhausted because not only did he have to keep himself psyched up, but he also had to keep Matt motivated not to quit. On the day of the marathon, Pete and Matt ran, Mark rode his bike alongside his brother, and I would meet them at different points to provide encouragement, band-aids, whatever was needed. Matt took his time and ran slower than Pete, and because I would wait for Matt at designated spots, I never saw Pete during the race. Pete finished that race before Matt; however, Pete came in looking like death warmed over, and Matt came across the finish line looking as fresh as when he started. Matt could never have run that marathon if not for his dad. Pete was always supportive of anything the boys and I did.

TIME FOR JUST THE TWO OF US

Pete and I were very competitive people with each other as well as with others. Pete could always beat me during a running race, but I could really whip him at racquet ball. Pete and I would go to the gym on Friday night and play racquet ball for hours. Pete tried so hard to beat me. He was so funny, running all over and trying to outdo me. I would be watching him and laughing so hard, I would have to stop playing. It was such fun for me. One night we were playing, and a tendon snapped in his calf. He insisted that I had purposely hit him with my racquet. I did not; however, he never believed me and always chose to tell everyone that I hit him with the racquet. His leg bothered him for several weeks and I don't think we ever did get back into racquet ball.

And then there were our date nights. During a class I was taking, the speaker talked about having date nights with her husband. She said that life was so busy, that she and her husband set aside one night a week that was just for them. Pete and I thought that sounded like something we would like. So we started having date nights on Wednesday evenings. I would pop the popcorn, take our sodas, and we would go to the movies. It was a nice evening for just the two of us. We thought we were pretty special; here we were married and still having date nights.

Not only did Pete and I love each other, we liked each other. We were friends. Early on in our marriage, I talked to Pete about how I thought marriage was just like a job—you had to work at it. I believe from the first time we had that talk, we did just that. We worked really hard at having a good marriage. You see people who have been married for a long time, sometimes even a short time, and they just exist in their relationship; there is no pizzazz. We were determined that it would not happen in our marriage. And it did not. Our marriage was full of excitement and surprises.

In September of 2000, Pete surprised me with what turned out to be our last vacation. While surfing the internet looking for paintings by a favorite painter of ours, Pete came across a weekend vacation in California centered on meeting the painter. Pete was really excited about this trip because it consisted of many activities of the Old West. Pete fancied himself as a western gunfighter. Of all the activities we attended, our favorites were panning for gold and watching a reenactment of a western gun fight. The conclusion of the weekend was a dinner with an opportunity to meet the painter. We were determined to get an autograph; actually, if you knew Pete and me, you would know that there was no way we were leaving without an autograph. Our painter not only attended the dinner, but brought his wife and four small daughters. Pete spent the entire evening getting autographs from our painter, his wife, and his four daughters. He managed to get all six autographs on the back of a small picture. Pete was so proud of the autographs. We enjoyed the weekend immensely. It made for good stories for him to tell.

PETE'S FUNNY STORIES

Pete could be very funny and tell the most outrageous stories. He loved to tell stories on himself. He would say it was just too good of a story to keep to himself. He would laugh until he had tears running down his face. Just watching him tell one of his stories provided so much enjoyment for those listening. He would always finish by wiping his eyes and saying, "That was a good one."

One of his stories included a mishap he had when he had a severe case of diarrhea. He told how he felt it coming on as he was driving down the street. He quickly pulled into a restaurant, ran to the bathroom, whipped down his pants, didn't quite get down on the seat before he had an "explosion." He told us that he "nailed" the entire toilet, floor, and the wall behind him. There was no way he could clean it up with just the toilet paper, so after telling the management that someone had made a mess in the bathroom, he left. He took great pleasure in telling us there was no way that the stall could be cleaned up without taking a hose to it. He said he could just visualize someone walking into that stall and seeing the mess. Thinking about that would always bring another round of laughter.

He also told a story about going to a massage therapist. Pete said that she was a little person, but strong as a gorilla. He said the pain she put him through was excruciating. He had to bite his lips to keep from screaming. He told how she would push down on his back until he was sure her hand was going to come out through his stomach. I had taken classes in reflexology and total body massage, but when I worked on Pete, I had to take it easy because I would hurt him. He might have called the massage therapist a gorilla but I knew that it was Pete who really was a wimp.

Another one of his stories was about rats. My brother owned a printing company and Pete was rewiring it for him. Very early one morning, Pete and Dick went to the printing company to start rewiring. They sat for awhile and enjoyed a cup of coffee until Dick decided it was time to start work. He went into a storage room and turned on the light and rats immediately ran for cover. Pete heard the noise and yelled "what the hell was that?" Dick laughed and told Pete it was rats. Pete then yelled "Holy crap" How big are they? They sounded like a team of Clydesdales."

TELLING ON PETE

I have my own funny stories involving Pete. One Halloween, I left our house and went to our neighbors.

My neighbor had a long fur coat. I stripped down to nothing and put on the coat and a scarf that covered my head and some of my face. I went back to our house and rang the doorbell. When Pete answered the door, I tore the coat open and just stood there. The look of shock on Pete's face was priceless. It took him a few seconds to recognize my body.

Around the time the boys were in high school, Pete and I started to go to Las Vegas every year. It was usually in March, which was during Lent. Pete, in addition to giving something up during Lent, always spent more time in prayer. He would spend one hour a day in church praying. Even while in Las Vegas he did this. One year while in Las Vegas, we found the church locked, so Pete decided he could pray for an hour sitting on the back stoop. Since I wasn't involved in his praying, I decided to get some walking in. I walked around and around the church. As I was passing by the front of the church, which was landscaped with heavy shrubbery, I heard a rustling in the shrubs and then I heard a voice. I screamed for Pete. About that time, the hobo in the shrubs said, "Quiet, lady, I'm trying to get some sleep." Pete came running around the church, scanned the situation and said to me, "Blankety-blank, what the hell is wrong with you? Can't you see I'm trying to pray?"

One of my favorite stories was when we went with our friends, Sondra and Franklin to an out-of -town funeral. At the end of the service, the priest told us to take our time and not hurry to our cars to go to the cemetery because the hearse and family cars would be going first. Well, Pete, who never liked to be late, rushed out, hurrying the rest of us. Pete took off from the parking lot, turned onto the main street, and we somehow found ourselves right behind the hearse. We were the first car in the funeral procession even before the entire family. Sondra, Franklin, and I were laughing so hard that we finally ducked down in the seats to keep people from seeing us laughing in a funeral procession line. Pete was on his own; he had made the mistake. He was in a panic and did not see any way out, so he followed the hearse. He pulled up to the cemetery right behind the hearse. We got out of the car, but soon found out Pete pulled up too close and the pall bearers could not get the casket out. Pete had to get back in the car and back up. That caused a chain reaction. The families of the deceased also had to return to their cars and back up. You can imagine how hard it was for Sondra, Franklin, and I to keep a straight face; Pete did not find the humor in it. Neither did the family of the deceased.

Pete went through a period of making boogers out of rubber cement. I don't know how he got started; perhaps a slow time at work. Anyway, when we were with other people, Pete would pretend to sneeze and stick the booger on his face so it looked like it was hanging out of his nose. It was gross, but you should have seen the reactions! People would immediately look away. Then they would look back for a second look as if to confirm what they saw. Finally, Pete and I couldn't take it any longer and would start laughing. We had one friend with a weak stomach who would dry heave. Even after she knew it was a trick, she would still dry heave. Pete used that little trick for several months.

Pete and I used to go to dances with a large group of parents from Matt and Mark's baseball team. Our friend, Judy McKinley also attended the dances. She was six feet tall and Pete was five feet four inches. Sometime during the course of the evening, Pete and Judy would dance to a slow song. He would lay his head on her breasts, get this blissful look on his face, and they would slowly sway to the music. Everyone there was watching and laughing. Another tradition was born.

GREEN BAY PACKERS

When Pete was a young child, he would spend his entire summer with relatives on a farm near Green Bay. Of course, he became a Green Bay Packer fan. I don't mean just a Packer fan, but a Packer fan! One summer, Pete and I drove up to Green Bay for a Packer's practice. At the end of the practice, the players would sign autographs. All the kids lined up with Pete pushing and shoving his way to the front of the line. Pete had bought a big poster and managed to get many autographs that day. He didn't care who he had to run over to get the autographs. I'm sure many parents wondered who that little man thought he was pushing and shoving their kids. That autographed poster is framed and hangs in our family room.

A Marriage of Giving

Pete was always my biggest cheerleader. No matter what I did, no matter how big or small, Pete was a constant source of encouragement. Sometimes, I would have to tone down his encouragement because it would become pressure for me. That is what happened when I started taking college classes. He started out okay, but soon began treating me like I was his child. He would make sure I did my homework and studied for my tests. It finally got to be a little too much for me, so we had to have a talk about his "encouragement." He pulled back and gave me some breathing room.

I have to tell you about our wedding anniversaries. Following his dad's tradition, Pete would get me one flower for each year we were married. He did this without fail. He was very specific that the number of flowers had to match the number of years we were married. As the years mounted up, it became harder for florists to make arrangements and keep to the right number of flowers. On our 23rd anniversary, Pete sent me 23 different colored carnations with baby's breath in a ruby colored vase. It was the most beautiful arrangement I had received. The next year Pete hired an acquaintance who had recently started a florist shop out of her home. That year the flower arrangement was very nice; however, the florist confessed that at a certain point, she lost track of the number of flowers, and thought, oh well, what the heck. That was the end of her; Pete never went back.

I was always doing silly, stupid things to shock and surprise Pete. If he were working out in the back-yard, I would knock on the window to get his attention and then flash him my bare chest. When it was Valentine's Day, I would make three paper hearts and stick them to my body. I was his Valentine's present.

My story would be missing something if I didn't tell you about the heart-shaped meat loaf I made each year for Pete. I read an article in a magazine about a young wife who didn't have the money to buy her husband anything for Valentine's Day, so she made him a heart-shaped meat loaf and wrote "I Love You" in ketchup. For Pete, there was something so special about me doing something so simple. He loved his meatloaf and would have been really hurt if I didn't make it. Heart-shaped meatloaves with "I Love You" written in ketchup became a tradition for us.

One summer weekend, Pete and I took a short trip to Door County, Wisconsin. On a Saturday, as we were coming back down the west side of the peninsula, Pete mentioned how we had to go to church. I whined a little and said, "Hey, we are on vacation, can't we miss it this time." I remember saying that I know when our friends are traveling, they don't go to church. Pete gave in and said we wouldn't look for a church; it would have to come to us. It was no more than five minutes later when we came across a Catholic Church that was just starting. Of course, we went to church! We sat in the third row on the right side. The church had a sky light, and just as we sat down, a bright ray of sunlight came through that sky light directly on Pete and me. We looked at each other and knew that God was pleased with us.

Pete sent me flowers quite frequently. There didn't have to be a special occasion, he just liked to send me flowers. The cards might say, "Just wanted to tell you I love you"; "Last night was special for us"; "I'm glad you are mine"; "You are mine forever"; just whatever was on his mind. When I started working at Rock Island High School, Pete would send me red and gold flowers because they were Rocky's school colors. He did this each year without fail. I worked there for over twenty years and each year on the first day of school, I had red and gold flowers on my desk.

Sometimes Pete would come in the back door from work and sing out "I got you a present." It could be something as small as a flavored bubble gum that I liked. If he saw something I liked, he usually got it for me. I did the same for him. We were always surprising each other with little presents. We both wanted that element of surprise in our marriage.

SOMETIMES WE DISAGREED

I don't want anyone to think that we were perfect and didn't have our disagreements, because we did. Sometimes we would get in an argument about something we both felt strongly about and not speak for several days. It was tormenting for both of us, but we both held our ground. We were both stubborn and thought we were right. Our usual pattern of sleeping at night would be for Pete to lie on his right side and I would cuddle up behind him. He would grab my arm and pull it around him. We always started the night wrapped around each other. On the nights we were not speaking, we would go to bed at night, sleeping apart, not touching, until we would accidently on purpose be close enough to each other to be touching. From there, it only got better.

RETIREMENT: WHAT TO DO

The years rolled by much too fast. We were both in our fifties. Our boys were grown and had their own lives. Pete and I talked about when we would retire and what we would do. We had no intention of working at another job. We were going to relax, play lots of golf, drink a few beers, enjoy spending time with family and friends, and just enjoy the life we had earned by all our years of hard work. Our life had run smoothly so far and we were looking forward to enjoying retirement. If we could have seen what the future held for us, we would have been terrified.

Symptoms Noticeable

It was during the summer of 2000 that I noticed Pete was different. He had always been a perfectionist with a Type A personality, but that was gone. He no longer had any ambition or drive. It never mattered to Pete whether he was doing his job at work or doing a project at home, everything he did had to be perfect. He had always taken such pride in our yard, but during that summer, he barely took care of it. I talked to him about it and he would just kind of laugh it off, like I was making too much of it. Nothing seemed to bother him.

Pete could not remember what day it was. There were days when he would dress to go to work, and I would tell him it was Saturday or Sunday. His secretary realized that something was very wrong and started writing out note cards for him as to what day it was and what he was supposed to be doing on that day. Pete never forgot my birthday or our anniversary, but during this time, he would send me a card on the wrong day and for the wrong occasion. Sometimes, he would realize he had been wrong.

In November, we were at a party with his family. His aunt asked him how long we had been married. When he answered, he was thirty years off. He looked at me and said, "That was wrong, wasn't it?" I remember riding home in the car and thinking that this is what our life would be from now on. We had been dealing with it for several months and I could see no way out. It was just going to continue and continue. I never once thought about a brain tumor. How could

I have been that stupid? I look back on those months and I can't believe that I didn't think of a brain tumor. I realize that it would not have made any difference, but to this day, I cannot believe I didn't think of it.

Pete had no concept of time. He would go somewhere and be gone for hours and wasn't aware of how long he was gone. One day I was at Matt's house waiting for Pete to come and install a light fixture. He arrived about three hours late. He came in with bags of flower seeds and bulbs that he had gotten for mere pennies. He was so happy with his bargain! He was not aware that he had been gone for so long. I would like to say that I was very patient with him, but I wasn't. I was frustrated; our life was so different and we were not making any headway. Nor were we getting any answers from the medical field. I look back with guilt at all the times that I wasn't patient or understanding, or thought he wasn't trying hard enough. It took me up until the time that he went into hospice before I realized that he just couldn't help it.

Pete was never late for work, for church, or almost anything, but he started to be late for everything. He had always waited on me to be ready to go somewhere and now I was waiting on him. When I talked to him about it, he once again just laughed it off. I realize now that he just couldn't understand it.

He was always falling asleep. If he sat down, he would sleep. Even at work, he would have to lie down and take a nap. He would fall asleep during meetings. One evening when we were at a work function,

I heard some of the guys making a joke about Pete falling asleep during meetings.

We both knew something was wrong. Pete had been going to his doctor for several months, but was not getting any answers. The doctor ran tests for different illnesses, but found nothing. A brain tumor was never considered. The doctor focused on sleep apnea and prescribed a sleep machine for Pete. This did not help and his symptoms grew worse. We would sit and talk about it, trying to figure out what was wrong. I thought he was depressed because he was turning sixty and was going to retire. He was afraid he had Parkinson's because his dad had it. We talked, and we talked, and we talked, and we couldn't come up with any answers. Pete always took showers, never a bath, but during this time, he would fill the tub with hot, bubbling water and ask me to join him. Almost every evening, we sat in the tub and tried to figure out what was wrong.

I finally talked him into seeing a psychiatrist. He went by himself the first time; however, I didn't feel he had explained everything to the doctor, so the second time I went with him. When we explained that his father had Parkinson's, the doctor made an appointment for Pete with a neurologist. I so clearly remember the day of that appointment. We were both so nervous, but at the same time, somewhat hopeful that we would find answers. I was in the examining room with Pete. After explaining to the doctor what Pete's symptoms were, the doctor first did a physical exam and then did some memory testing. At the conclusion, he told us that Pete did not have Parkinson's. We were so happy; we thought God had answered our prayer. You know the saying, be careful what you ask for? That came home to us. We had asked God for Pete not to have Parkinson's, and within a few days, found out he had a condition that was so much worse.

The doctor said to be on the safe side, he would order an MRI of Pete's brain. We were sent to the secretary to schedule the test with the hospital. There were no openings for about a month, and then, even while we stood there, an opening came up the next day. A day after the MRI on the brain, Pete had a telephone message from the doctor's office to come in at 8:00 a.m. the next day with his wife. I knew it had to be very bad news—Pete was oblivious of the meaning. We spent the evening at the hospital because our grandchild was going to be born. Pete took his camera and took pictures. I found out later that he didn't have any film in the camera. We stayed at the hospital until our granddaughter, Morgan Christine Mander, was born early the next day, December 7, 2000. It turned out to be the same day that we got the news that forever changed our life.

PETE'S DIAGNOSIS

DECEMBER 7, 2000

Pete's doctor's appointment was at 8:00 a.m. He was so tired that I had a hard time getting him out of bed. We finally got to the doctor's office about 8:45 a.m. The doctor came into the examining room with another person, who he introduced as a doctor. I didn't have to be told to know that it was truly bad. The doctor showed us the x-ray. It was easy to see the big white spot, which was a tumor. He went on to explain that this tumor was terminal, there was no cure, and Pete had about six months to live. It was that quick! The neurologist made an appointment for Pete to see a neurosurgeon within the hour. Then the two doctors left us alone. It was only then that the tears started to come. As I cried, I looked over to Pete, who was starting to get dressed. He had tears running down his face. I couldn't speak. We couldn't even touch each other. The doctor, in just a few seconds, had taken our life away and had not given us any hope. I cannot come up with the words to explain what I felt like. We didn't know what to say or do; we didn't even know how to comfort each other. We were zombies! We were numb!

We went to see the neurosurgeon. He confirmed what the neurologist had said. There wasn't any hope, Pete was going to die. Both the neurologist and the neurosurgeon pretty much said it just that way. There was no sugar coating anything. In a matter of an hour, two men stripped away our life.

Surgery was scheduled for the following week at Genesis in Davenport, Iowa. We left the surgeon's office to go to the hospital for tests so Pete could have the surgery. I cannot explain the fear I had that day. We had been told Pete was going to die—they did not give us any hope at all. That was the worst day of my life. Fear had paralyzed us. I don't know how we got through that day, but we did.

TELLING OUR SONS

When we got home in the late afternoon, I called our daughter-in-law with the news. I asked her to reach our sons, Matt and Mark, and have them both come to our house. I asked her not to tell them anything; it was something I was going to have to do. Mark came first and I told him. I try to remember his reaction and I can't. I think he just walked away like it could not be true—just Mom overreacting again. Then Matt walked in and I told him. I remember so well Matt crying and saying to me, "But Mom, he isn't going to die, is he?"

Pete had fallen asleep in his chair. I sat on the sofa. Matt came to the sofa and huddled next to me and Mark sat at my feet. We were so lost. They were my babies again and I didn't know how to help them.

GETTING A SECOND OPINION

The next day, our friends, Jolene and Jack advised us to get a second opinion. We took their advice and got an appointment in Iowa City. The boys, Pete, and I went for the appointment. This doctor was much, much kinder and did give us a glimmer of hope, but was pretty positive the tumor was a glioblastoma, which had about a .5 percent recovery rate. He said he would do surgery to take out as much of the tumor as he could, and then Pete would follow up with six weeks of radiation. Pete and I were both very emotional. I explained to the surgeon that Pete's biggest fear was that he would be in a vegetative state. The doctor said he would take as much of the tumor as he could without causing brain damage to Pete.

SURGERY

Pete had surgery on December 13, 2000. After surgery, the surgeon confirmed the type of tumor and told us it was malignant. He explained that he had removed as much as he could; however, he did not get all of it. He said radiation might help destroy the rest. This doctor never took our hope away from us.

Pete spent three days in the hospital. I stayed at the hospital with him; I could not leave him. The day after the surgery, the head of the radiology department came into Pete's room and, looking at his clipboard, told us that Pete would have six weeks of radiation and the average life span of a person with this tumor was six months. All of this was said in a monotone, just like he was reciting. The doctor showed no emotion, sympathy, or compassion at all. Pete did not understand what the doctor had said. He chose to believe that they had gotten the entire tumor and he was going to be all right.

Recovery and Fear

We came home much sooner than I thought he should. We didn't know what we were doing or how he should be feeling and we were here and the doctor was in Iowa City. Pete felt terrible and looked terrible. We were scared. We talked about his dying and what would happen to me. We knew where he was going, but I would be left without him.

Radiation started December 28, 2000. We had many people rally around us. I think I took him to radiation only about five times because he always had a few pals to take him. The regulars were Tim Lavell, Ed Kenney, and Mike Kavanagh. They would drive up to Iowa City, Pete would have his radiation, and then they would go to breakfast. Pete enjoyed his breakfasts with the guys. We were being pro-active and it felt good. We started praying together each day. Pete was always so private with his prayer life, but I told him we had to pray together and we did. We decided to fight this thing.

SUPPORT AND ADVICE

Our friends, Jack and Jolene, and Franklin and Sondra stayed close to us and kept us busy. The six of us had a prayer service and anointed Pete with oil and sprinkled him with holy water. We all went to a healing mass and ended up having a good time that night. We sat in the front pew so we could see everything. People would line up at the altar railing. The priest would move from person to person, say something, and touch their forehead. Most of the people would fall backward. There were helpers there to catch them. I guess none of the six of us received the healing because we didn't fall backward. Afterward, we went out for pizza and found great enjoyment in discussing the healing mass.

RADIATION TREATMENT

Pete and I followed advice from everyone on prayer, anointing, thanking God for his healing, everything that we could. I asked everyone to pray. I was building up an army of people who would pray. I was practically tackling people on the street to ask them to pray. There was nothing I wouldn't do—I was going to beat this cancer. I was going to make Pete live.

After radiation ended, we hit a slump. Now we were waiting and not taking an active role. That was not a good feeling. We continued our prayers and kept believing we were going to beat cancer. After all, God told us if we ask for anything in his name, it will be granted. I took those words literally. God said it, so it was going to be.

We met with an oncologist to discuss chemotherapy. The doctor told us that it wouldn't do any good to have chemo. The tumor was very aggressive and terminal. Again, someone who didn't give us any hope. I did not like this guy. I felt like the doctors were playing God! They had no right to tell us Pete was doing to die without giving us some hope. No one decides when someone is going to die except God.

During one of Pete's appointments with his radiologist, I asked the doctor to do a complete body scan on Pete to check if there was cancer anywhere else. The doctor explained to us that this type of tumor only grew on the brain. It was during that meeting that I told the doctor that I didn't want to hear any more about a terminal illness or Pete dying. I told him that we needed to have hope and that we were going to fight. I told him that only God could decide when Pete would die. From that day on, we developed a good relationship with the radiologist and he became our friend. I like to think that Pete and I made an impression on him, and that his future patients would know a more compassionate doctor who just didn't rattle off statistics.

FEELING LOST

After radiation ended, Pete had a few good months of being his old self. He went back to work, tried running a little, and because he felt pretty decent, thought he had beaten the cancer. In April, he had an additional massive dose of radiation. After that, I could see a decline. The old symptoms were coming back. I read and read on this disease and found out that the radiation could make him have the symptoms, so I chose to believe it was the radiation. I lived each day in fear. Fear was my life!

• • •

Pete and I tried to lead our life as normal as possible. In June, 2001, Barb and Joel took us to Chicago for a weekend to see a Cubs game. When we returned on a Sunday evening, we had a phone message from Ed Kenney's daughter. We called her and she explained that Ed had been diagnosed with a brain tumor, a glioblastoma, the same tumor as Pete's. We all found this alarming and wondered if Ed had contracted the tumor from Pete. In speaking with Pete's radiologist, we were told that it was just a coincidence. The doctor said there was absolutely no connection. We were relieved but still wondered.

On July 4, 2001, God blessed us with another granddaughter, Madison Kay Mander. Pete and I were both at the hospital when she was born. Even though our whole family was living under extreme stress, we still had reason to celebrate and thank God. When we left the hospital, Pete called my mom. His words were, "We have a new granddaughter. Now we have two patriotic granddaughters." Morgan was born on December 7, 2000—Pearl Harbor Day, and Madison was born July 4, 2001—Independence Day.

Cancer Growing

By mid-July, I just knew that the cancer was growing again; however, a brain scan at Iowa City indicated that the tumor had shrunk. But, only days after that report, Pete got much worse. By the end of the summer, he was pretty much immobile and needed care.

Let Go, Let God

On September 8, 2001, our son Mark, my brother Dick, his wife Cyndi and I took Pete to Iowa City to his radiologist. Pete was in a wheel chair, almost comatose. He could do nothing—it was the worst he had been. The radiologist did an MRI and said it showed tumor growth; it was not necrosis or radiation damage. He said Pete could have another surgery to remove some of the tumor and give him a few more good months, or we could make him comfortable and not have any more treatment. That day, we, collectively, decided no more treatment. It was time to let go and let God.

BEGINNING OF HOSPICE

We brought Pete home that day. He slept the whole way and was unaware of what we had just found out. For me, that hour and a half riding home was pure hell. My Pete was going to leave me. He was going to die. How could I live without him? I thought about Heaven and what it was like and what Pete would be doing there. Pete had been such an active person; I didn't want him being bored in Heaven. Oh, the thoughts that went through my mind. It was more than I could bear that I was going to lose Pete. We had lost the battle.

The next day, I contacted Pathway Hospice. They came to our home and explained the program. They insisted that Pete be included in the discussion, so we sat at the kitchen table with Pete. He did not understand what was happening. His mind would not let him.

A hospital bed was delivered to our home on September 11, 2001. We put the bed in the eating area that adjoined the family room. I could not put him in a bedroom away from everyone. He had to be in the center of everything. He was still ours and we were not going to shut him away. He was ours to take care of, and we had to do a good job. Everything had to be for Pete. We needed to do everything right, because that's what Pete would have done for us.

Started Journal

On the day that Pete started hospice, I started a journal. I am giving it to you as I have written it, with very few changes. So many times, as I was writing, I thought, people need to read this, people need to know what it's like to go through this, and I need to help others. As you read it, you will find that I wasn't always kind to those who I felt had failed us, but, those were and actually still are my true feelings. I wrote as I felt at that moment. I didn't hold anything back. I screamed, I cried, I gave myself up to my feelings. I hope, as you read it, you will be able to put yourself in my place. The journal will make you cry, but it will also make you laugh. It will make you sad, but it will also give you hope. It will make you realize that no matter what happens in your life, you can get through it because God is with you. I give you my most personal thoughts in my journal.

MY JOURNAL

TUESDAY, SEPTEMBER 11, 2001

In December, when we learned Pete had cancer, a few people told me to keep a journal. I did not. Now I wished I had—the past nine months have been a total blur. I can't redo the past nine months of not writing, but I can start my journal today, the first day of hospice for Pete.

Now we are at the end. We fought and fought and now our battle is over. It is up to God, as we know it has always been.

At this point and for the last two weeks, Pete is almost totally incapacitated. He cannot walk or feed himself, and barely speaks—his mind won't let him. He does understand a few things, but cannot respond when he wants to. He can laugh at certain things and he usually responds to Matt and Mark.

Today he started with the Hospice Program. They came and set up the bed. He has been sleeping in the lounge chair for a couple weeks. I don't know what he understands about what is happening to him. I do try to talk to him. Today he cried, but I think he was confused. I think he thought the World Trade Buildings were actually the Rock Island Arsenal. When Mark came in dressed in fatigues, Pete cried again. Mark hugged him and said "Dad, I'm alright—that's in New York." We babysat Madison today. Grandpa held her and she was good. We were going to have Morgan, Madison, and our grandson Ian baptized at home, but had to cancel because of Mark working. Matt and Morgan came tonight, Morgan sat on Grandpa's lap and I fed them blueberry yogurt, one bite for Morgan and one bite for Grandpa.

I don't know if Pete knows where he is in the dying process. I talked to him and asked him if he was afraid; he said "no." I told him we were lucky to have had thirty-seven years of marriage and two great sons. I told him he was lucky he was going home to be with God and he would be met by Jeff. I told him he was going to be with Jeff and I would stay here and take care of the boys until it was time for me to join him.

WEDNESDAY, SEPTEMBER 12, 2001

The hospice nurse came today. She talked with Pete, checked him out. I walked out with her. I told her I needed to know when the end was coming. She said she didn't know if she could tell me. She said sometimes with this tumor, you just go to sleep. She said it could be over any day or could last for a few months.

I bought cemetery plots today, four of them at Calvary. I made arrangements for Jeff to be moved. He will be buried at the feet of Pete. I talked with Matt and told him he and Mark needed to talk with our priests about the funeral. I will call Foht's on music and get flowers. The boys will go to the funeral home and make arrangements. SueAnn called tonight and cannot come to visit Pete. We had a nice talk. Pete's mother called; she asked if I had gotten any help yet. I said yes and she asked if I could handle it. Again, I said yes. I told her I had the boys, friends and neighbors, my sister was coming for two weeks, my brother had been here twice to stay a few days, and my mom was coming to help me. She said she would like to help, but she had to take care of Dad. She said that she could come, but she would have to bring Dad. I asked her not to as it would be too much for her and for me.

THURSDAY, SEPTEMBER 13, 2001

Sondra and Franklin came today. We had a nice visit. Pete was a little responsive. He was able to say a few words to them. Diane Kavanagh stopped by with her nephew. How wonderful it is to have people who care about us and support us. Thank you, God.

FRIDAY, SEPTEMBER 14, 2001

Sister Charlotte came today. She said she would be stopping in a few times a week and would bring communion for us on Fridays. She told me that she had heard wonderful stories about Pete and his devotion to God. She had even heard the story about our vacation in Door County when God touched us with his light.

Tim and Karen Lavell stopped by for a visit. It was obvious that it was very hard for Tim to see Pete the way he was. For once, Tim was at a loss for words.

Geri came with dresses for the babies to wear for their baptism. I called her and asked her to buy the dresses, and boom, she was there with what I needed.

SATURDAY, SEPTEMBER 15, 2001

Pete woke up more alert—he asked me to get in bed with him—I did. He said he thought he would like to go out to lunch today. I got him cleaned up and we thought together we could get him into the wheelchair. We could not. He ended up on the floor. I called Barb and asked her to come down to help. We still couldn't get the job done, so Barb asked one of the construction men working in the neighborhood to help. They finally got him in the wheelchair and outside. He was outside a couple hours. We walked three laps around the neighborhood, not going down hills.

When we got him back in, he took a long nap, had supper and some time in there I sensed a real change in his mood—depressed. Hope, Kathy, and my mom called to check. His back hurt during the night. I tried to move him to his side a little, got into bed with him for a short while. Ron Foht stopped by today.

SUNDAY, SEPTEMBER 16, 2001

Pete woke up still depressed but alert. I fed him breakfast; he was falling asleep during breakfast. I am sitting here writing this and he says, "What are you doing?" The boys are coming around 5:00 p.m. and we will get him in the shower.

The boys and I wheeled Pete to bathroom and undressed him. They put him in the shower then I got in with him and washed him. The boys are wonderful with their dad. They are digging deep and doing things that are difficult.

Terrill was here for a short visit. Told Pete he loved him. Sondra and Franklin came in the evening; I made chocolate/peanut butter cake.

MONDAY, SEPTEMBER 17, 2001

Waited all day for home health aide; no one came. I called hospice; they did not have us scheduled. They will come tomorrow, Wednesday at the latest. Jolene called. She told me last Monday night they would come every night to help me get Pete in bed. I haven't seen her since. I told her that she said that; she said she had a busy week. Life goes on for everyone else; it has stopped for me. I pray that I won't be bitter. Geri came after work. Barb came and brought fish and fries for us. Between the three of us, we got Pete in the wheelchair and took him for a walk. When I got Pete ready for bed last night, we missed the bed. I thought I could get him out of the wheelchair. I couldn't. He ended up on the floor. I called Matt. He came out and we got him in bed. Pete still tells the boys, "Be careful" when they leave.

TUESDAY, SEPTEMBER 18, 2001

Hospice nurse came with student nurse. They helped me change Pete. A really good day for Pete. Jack and Franklin and Sondra came over in the evening. Jack brought Pete a Packer's cap. Jolene had a book club meeting.

WEDNESDAY, SEPTEMBER 19, 2001

Maitlens came. Gene put up bird feeder and fixed cable outlet in bedroom. Matt and Morgan were here. Morgan is such a joy, she makes my life better. She kept laughing out loud and making noises. She really put on a show. Matt grilled steaks. I fried potatoes and onions—great supper. Grandpa and Morgan shared a yogurt. A nurse's aide came today to clean Pete up. She was so gentle, not like me.

THURSDAY, SEPTEMBER 20, 2001

The Hospice Chaplain came today. She and I talked for about an hour. She wanted to know how we were all handling Pete's sickness. I told her about the close relationship of Pete and Ian, and that I was most concerned about Ian. She said it would be a good idea for her to talk with Ian.

WEDNESDAY, OCTOBER 11, 2001

The days go by, one running into another. I'll try to catch up. Talked with Ian about Grandpa. He asked me if Grandpa was getting better because his voice was louder. I told Ian that Grandpa was very sick and might not get better. Ian said, "I know, he's getting ready to go to Heaven." Ian realizes a lot. He knows Grandpa isn't the same. He always hugs him good-bye, but I'm not sure if he wants to or thinks he is supposed to. He will feed Pete, give him drinks, and take care of him. He saw a younger picture of Pete and said, "That was when Grandpa was new. Now he looks old." Ian asked Mark if some day Mark would be a grandpa. Mark said "yes." Ian then asked if Grandma and Grandpa look different now than when they used to. Mark said, "No, they look the same." Ian said "No, Grandpa doesn't have hair on top and he looks old."

Phil and Ruthie surprised us one Friday with a visit. Madison was here and Phil fell in love with her. That blonde hair and blue eyes really did a number on him. It was nice that Hope was here too and they got to see her. We ordered pizza for lunch. I enjoyed being with my family.

Hope has been here two weeks and is leaving tomorrow. She has been wonderful. She has taken care of both me and Pete. The boys and their families have been here a lot. Hope has enjoyed seeing all of them.

I called Ruthie and asked her to come and stay with me, but she is still working.

Kathy and Jim brought Mom and Dad Saturday. No word from Bill or Rick. SueAnn wrote a letter to Pete. In the letter, she explained that she wouldn't be able to come to see him. She told him that she would see him in Heaven. I did not read that part of the letter to Pete.

Dick and Cyndi and my mom come every two weeks. Cyndi has offered to come and stay with us.

I asked Pete's mom to come and stay with us awhile. I told her to have Dad stay with Kathy or Rick. She said she couldn't leave him because she knows what he needs.

The Maitlens are great. Geri usually comes three times a week. She said she finally realized I wouldn't ask for anything, so now she just comes.

Brunsvolds are always there for us. They understand what we are going through. The Youngs are a puzzle—we do not hear from them at all—for months. I do not understand.

What can I say about Matt and Mark? They have both gone beyond anything I thought they were capable of. The touching and affection and patience and love they show Pete cannot be explained. They are doing things for him (toilet duties, dressing) and they are doing it with love, respect, and humor.

Me, I live in fear each day. Even though I try to plan for what I know is inevitable, I do not know how I'm going to go through it. I look at Pete and I am so sad he is going through this. He isn't Pete; he just exists. I broke down with him one day; he asked me why I was crying and I said, "Because you are so miserable." He said "You are miserable too." One day, as I was cleaning him, he looked up at me and said, "It takes a lot of love to do this." I wonder how I am going to live without him. He has always been my strength; he has always taken care of me. Now I have to be strong and take care of him. My fear is so great; how will I live without him. How am I going to bury him? How am I going to let him go? Who will touch me, who will tell me they love me, who will ever be as good to me as Pete? Who will spoil me like Pete? Who will support me like Pete? Who will I talk to at night? How will I live alone?

THURSDAY, OCTOBER 12, 2001 3:30AM

This is my third time to be up tonight; Pete has been sleeping each time. That is good. When I wake up during the night, I think Pete is in bed with me. Or sometimes I think I am going to see him walk into our bedroom. I have to get my strength from God. I have to hold on to that thought. I also have to think Pete is going away for awhile and I will join him later. After he is gone, I need him to come back to me so I can feel his presence.

Santamans and Morellis came over last night. Jack is going to retire and offered to come and stay with Pete a few hours while I go out. I will do that. Jack can be good at taking care of him.

Talked with Henrietta. Ed is still mobile, but very forgetful. He has been "hyper" from the beginning. He never stops talking or asking questions. She needs help; she needs someone in that house to take the pressure off her.

Tonight we see our Morgan. What joy she brings into our life.

SATURDAY, OCTOBER 14, 2001

Pete's parents and Kathy and Jim came today and stayed about two hours. When they left, Dad leaned down and said something to Pete. I don't know what was said, but Pete was crying. I know for the past several years, he is always upset after seeing his dad. Laura brought Ian and Madison over. Matt was here.

SUNDAY, OCTOBER 15, 2001

Pete woke up pretty clear headed. I asked him if he wanted to go to McDonald's. He said "yes." I asked him twice more and he still said "yes." I told him he would have to be in the wheelchair and he said it was okay with him if it was with me. Then I found out the wheelchair doesn't fold up. When Matt came over, I fed Pete, and then went to K-Mart and the grocery store. Later, after Mark came, both boys helped me with Pete in the bathroom. I gave him a shower. It is so pathetic to see him so helpless and the three of us taking care of him. He has always taken care of us. The boys are marvelous. After dinner, I brought Ian in my bedroom and read him a children's book about Heaven. I told him Grandpa might not get well and would go to Heaven. He did not say anything or ask any questions, but I think he understands very well. I think he has distanced himself from Pete. I reminded him of all the things he and Grandpa did together, plant grass seed, mow the lawn, pee in the bushes. I told him those were the things that make up Grandpa's soul and that's what would go to Heaven. When we were all done, he looked at the ceiling and asked why we had two smoke detectors. I think he heard every word I read and said, but didn't want to acknowledge it. He has a way of ignoring what he doesn't want to deal with. I hate it so much that Ian won't have Pete. They were so close. Ian needed Pete. And my babies will grow up without their grandpa. My tears flow so freely. I hurt for more than just me.

FRIDAY, OCTOBER 19, 2001

Running the sweeper in the bedroom. I always think Pete's going to get up and walk to me. I will miss him so much.

SUNDAY, OCTOBER 21, 2001

Went to Candi's wedding last night. Matt stayed with Pete and then the Maitlens relieved him. I'm not sure if he even knew I was gone. I have been walking more this past week. I can do a lot of thinking and I cry—a good release. I am so concerned about my weight—silly, I know, with what I'm going through, but I want to look good for the funeral. I want everything perfect for Pete. The boys have both gotten their suits. I have a black suit, but it is too small. I have to lose twenty pounds to wear it, but I keep eating.

Pete's body (limbs) is wasting away. The flesh just hangs on his arms and legs. Matt and I gave him a shower yesterday. It has to feel good. He used to love just sitting in the shower. It's nice to get his hair washed. I put baby oil on his body and Vaseline on his feet. His skin is so dry. I keep expecting him to walk into a room or when I'm walking by the house, I expect him to come out. Sometimes, something will happen and I can hardly wait to share it with Pete, then I realize he won't understand or enjoy it like he used to. I miss that so much.

I would like to get people to stay with Pete in the mornings so I can go to work. I know Diane Kavanagh said she would. I think Frannie is taking over my job.

SATURDAY, OCTOBER 27, 2001

When I wake up at night, I still think Pete is next to me. And, I keep thinking he is going to walk into the room. I think, think, and think—about everything. My thoughts never stop. I am so grateful for the time we as a family have had together this past year. It has given the boys the opportunity to reach out and care for their dad. My boys are amazing. All three of us have found something in ourselves we didn't know we had. The boys will take care of me and I will take care of them.

The Maitlens are wonderful. They come two to three times a week. It is amazing what you see and find during a time like this. I see Gene in a different way. He seems very devoted to helping us. He and Geri are both comfortable in helping with Pete.

People are strange. Some that you expect to be here are not and those you least expect rise up to the situation.

The Youngs—what gives? I don't think they want to be around us. I can't figure it out. Don is worried about his back? Maybe they are uncomfortable? They have been through this before with another friend, so they shouldn't be uncomfortable. I do not ask for their help unless I have to.

I am fixated on the visitation and funeral. I want everything to be perfect. I want the boys and me to make Pete proud. I think about the obit and want it to say what a truly great person Pete was, but I don't know what to say.

Pete's mom called last night, had been two weeks since she was here. She wants to come here for Thanksgiving and spend the night. That is another four weeks away. I would like for her to come and spend some time with Pete.

Pete had a good day today. Thank you, God. He held Madison for the longest time tonight. She slept in his arms. He kept stroking her face, head, and hands. We are so blessed, what joy the babies have brought.

SUNDAY, OCTOBER 28, 2001

Another good day for Pete. Matt came and we got Pete into the shower. Spaghetti for dinner. Brunsvolds here in p.m.

TUESDAY, OCTOBER 30, 2001 4:30 A.M.

I lay here and think and think. How lucky the boys and I are to have Pete this past year. We are able to take care of him and let him know how much we love him. I hope he understands what's going on. I'm not sure. I want to be with him when his soul leaves his body. I want to feel it. Now that winter is coming, I hope he waits until spring. I don't want to bury him in the winter. The boys and I will have to make Jeff's grave blanket. Pete has always done it and put such care and love in it. Even last year after the diagnosis, he still made the blanket. I always remember Pete and Johnny making a grave blanket for my dad the first year, and then Johnny lay under it.

Dick and Cyndi coming today. Dick is going to wire my basement. He will leave this weekend, but Cyndi will stay another two weeks. I will be able to work half days. If Pete should get worse, I would stay home with him.

TUESDAY, OCTOBER 30, 2001 9:00 P.M.

Not a good day for Pete. Didn't talk much and wasn't really good with it. Dick and Cyndi came, they are so good. Matt here tonight. Matt and I took Pete to bathroom. Pete couldn't sit up straight, leaning against the wall. Matt is so good. He says, "Dad, are you hurting? You would tell me, wouldn't you? Dad, I won't let you fall, you know that don't you?" Matt put his socks and pajama bottoms on him, talking to him the whole time. Green Bay Packer socks, pretty snazzy. I lost it. Later, Matt held me and rubbed my back and he lost it. Pete is going to die and there is nothing we can do. I don't know how I can handle the end.

FRIDAY, NOVEMBER 2, 2001

This morning, as I was changing Pete, he reached up to me. I took his hand and placed it on my chest and said, "You have my heart." As I thought about it later,

I knew that what I said was true. Pete was going to take a part of my heart with him and I would never be whole again.

SUNDAY, NOVEMBER 3, 2001

Another weekend gone. Had everyone here. Pete pretty much the same. I am so sad he is so sick. I told him that this morning and asked him if he was sad. He said "a little." He said something like it wouldn't be bad except for the tears. Yes, I was crying, but I am big on tears and he knows it. We have lived with this for more than a year. Pete started having symptoms in July, 2000, and was diagnosed December 7, 2000.

MONDAY NOVEMBER 4, 2001

I don't know how I will ever be able to let Pete go. What will I do without him to touch and to be touched? What will I do without his, "I love you." I cry and I hurt and I'm so sad. The tears roll down my face. I can hardly stand seeing him this way. No retirement to enjoy. How am I ever going to make it through this life without him? I wish I knew more about Heaven. I hope God lets Pete come visit me in a way that I know Pete is near. I ask God for strength and courage and the ability to accept his will, but I am still so afraid.

The boys and I have decided to stay with Father Tommy for the funeral. We all like him and feel good about him. He and Sister Charlotte are taking care of us.

FRIDAY, NOVEMBER 9, 2001

Had negative experience with hospice nurse. She said Pete got mad at her and had an attitude. Cyndi and the health care aide did not think so. The aide told me to ask for a different nurse. I said I'll wait.

Maitlens here today. Gene has come a long way. He held Pete's hand when he left. I cried. When someone shows him affection, I cry. Joel came to put him in bed. Joel kissed him and told him he loved him. Pete said, "I love you too." I cried. What am I ever going to do without Pete?

Pete was "on" tonight. When he reaches for me to touch me, he is "on." We have so much to be thankful for. Help me to remember to give thanks. Give me strength and courage to go on.

SATURDAY, NOVEMBER 10, 2001

Cyndi has been with us for two weeks. What a blessing. She is so good with Pete. She is there for his every need, mine too. She is such a good person. She takes care of everything she can so she won't bother me with it.

When I look at Pete and he is looking at me, I try and look so deep in his eyes so we will always have that connection. I need that connection to surpass death.

When I think about Pete going to Heaven, I think about my friend Pam. I loved her so much and have been at such a loss since she died. The last thing she said to me was, "Tell Petey, hey." Now she will be able to tell him hey herself.

MONDAY, NOVEMBER 12, 2001

Went to doctor today. I went for many reasons. I needed to touch base to renew Zoloft and Xanax. I always call in and they give me what I want, so I felt I should go in. Also went for her to check my arm; it hurts most of the time. She gave me samples to try. She talked to me about Pete. She asked me if I was ready to let go of Pete. How do you ever get ready? No, I'm not ready. How will I ever do without him? He has been my life, my strength, what will I do when I don't have him to touch? How did this happen? I was supposed to die first.

Frannie told me how she acted when her husband died. She said she thought she was ready but she screamed and grabbed him. He opened his eyes. The nurse made her leave the room until she could control herself. If I am there when Pete dies, I don't think I'll be able to let him go. I cry and cry and think and think. I'm getting nowhere. He is going to die.

TUESDAY, NOVEMBER 27, 2001 4:30AM

I am going to work today for a.m. Mark has day off and will stay with Pete. I have become a bitter, resentful person. I resent those who I feel have failed us. They have abandoned us. They just go on with their lives and forget about us. I would never do that to them and neither would Pete. I don't know how to deal with it. Am I being unfair?

Pete is not talking much now. Although last night, Geri was getting ready to leave and we decided to get him into bed from the chair. It took us a while to even figure out how to move him, but we finally got him (kind of) in the chair. We got him to the bed and started to put him in the bed and he said, "Somehow I don't have much confidence in this." That was the longest sentence he had said in days. He was smiling and found the whole situation funny, as did Geri and I.

I stayed home with him yesterday. No one to come in. I got in bed with him twice and just laid there and touched and stroked him. It's winter now. How am I going to put him in the ground? I look so deep into his eyes. I want him to read what's in my soul. I want a connection that he can take with him. I still don't understand how a body is no longer a body.

Everyone tells me how brave I am. I do not think so. I worry so much about the end. I do not think I can do it. How is a person no longer a person? Is he going to carry me with him?

Tonight Maitlens are coming over and we are having ham and beans and cornbread.

THURSDAY, NOVEMBER 30, 2001

Stayed home with Pete yesterday. When I got up and looked at him, he just looked so bad. He wasn't connecting with me at all. He was quiet all day, not really speaking at all. Matt and Morgan came last night. We still didn't get anything out of Pete. I decided to stay home again today. He didn't want to wake up this morning. I had a hard time getting him to eat and drink. Are we coming toward the end? I am not going to be able to handle this. I asked God for strength. Today is not a good day for me. I was up half the night—thinking, thinking, and thinking.

SUNDAY, DECEMBER 2, 2001

Almost a year since the diagnosis. My biggest fears. How do I separate Pete's body from Pete? I know it's just a shell, but it's my shell. How can he one second be alive and the next dead. Don't think I can handle the end. Probably would be best to find him. Second biggest fear, how to get through visitation (long, long line) and funeral? Can't see myself doing it. Probably all of that will be easy compared to being alone after he's gone. I'm not going to be a couple. I won't be invited to things.

I feel so hurt by Santamans and Morellis. What happened to them? We need them and they aren't here. I feel so alone without them. We had so many years of fun, friendship, and laughter, and now very little. They just don't get it. It's like suck it up and deal with it. They seem to think it's their duty to come out every two weeks. I can't believe they can't find the time once a week.

Pete was better yesterday. Even made a few comments about Morgan. Some days he is totally out of it and others more alert.

SUNDAY, DECEMBER 9, 2001

A whole week has gone by since I wrote. Not a good week for Pete. I stayed home Monday. Dick and Cyndi brought my mom up to stay. I went to work Tuesday and Wednesday. When I got home Wednesday, the aide was here. Pete was not doing well. He was coughing a lot and choking on the phlegm. He was so tired. Aide was concerned. I cried and cried.

The end is closer and I can't bear it. I can't bear a life without Pete. It seems he has been this way so long; this is the way I know him, not as he was. I miss the communication so much, just the looks without saying anything. Things happen that we would just love together, but he doesn't understand. I can hardly wait to tell him about some funny incident, and then I remember, he doesn't understand. I miss that connection so much.

After a bad Wednesday, I stayed home Thursday and Friday. My mom is doing a great job with Pete. It is good for her, more activity than she has had in years. She thinks it's pretty cool that sometimes he'll talk to her and not me. Pete would enjoy that.

Pete's Mom called on Wednesday. Asked how things were going. Not good. They were coming up on the sixteenth, maybe they should come earlier. She said she would feel bad if anything happened and she hadn't seen Pete. She said this is so hard for me. She said Dad still wasn't too good, got confused. She called the next day. Rick was bringing them Sunday.

Friday brought Father Tommy, social worker from hospice, and Tanya brought Morgan on her birthday. It has been one year ago today that we got the diagnosis on Pete. I thought about the day and the fear we had. That day is too hard to explain. The fear now is different, a more calm kind of fear. I love Pete so much; we just look at each other. I know what I am thinking, but what is he thinking? What a devastating illness, to take a vibrant person like Pete and make him into a totally helpless individual who can't even think.

Ian stayed over Saturday. I talked to him about Grandpa and his illness. I tried to be honest and explain exactly what had happened to Grandpa and how it affected his brain. I told Ian that Grandpa was going to die, but he already knew that. I told him to remember how close the two of them were and all the things they did together. I told him he would see Grandpa again when Ian died. Ian was very quiet while I talked. I cried as I talked and he just listened. I told him he would always be our favorite grandson.

. . .

Sunday, Rick brought Mom and Dad. Kathy and Jim came and brought Aunt Patsy, wasn't expecting them. Dad was doing really great. They came about 11:00 a.m. and left at 2:00 p.m. Kathy and Jim left about 3:30 p.m. Kathy sat by Pete and talked to him. Jim helped when he was coughing. His mom told him she would send some cookies. I asked Jim to do a reading at the funeral. He told me what a good job I was doing. He told me to watch for Pete's feet to turn dark. That was a sign the end was near.

When Mark was leaving tonight, he was saying good-bye to Pete, and Pete pipes up with "I love you, Mark." That helped Mark. Laura gave Pete a hug good-bye. How long God?

DECEMBER 11, 2001 2:30AM

Woke up second time already. Pete is sleeping. Saw Ann Mulvey today. She has been so good to send cards. She has mellowed over the years; she cried and hugged me.

I have a little cold, think I gave it to Pete. Not a great day for him yesterday. Some days I don't get him to speak at all. I miss our communication most of all. The things we could tell each other or just the looks and we would understand. I keep trying to tell him things I know he would understand, but I am not getting a response. Oh, how I miss that. I look so deeply into his eyes, but I can't read anything. I found a picture of him from work taken about three years ago—a great picture. But, that person no longer exists. I can't believe the change. It has crept up so slowly. I didn't realize until I saw the picture. I have been told that once this is all over, I will remember Pete as he was when he was healthy. I hope so, because now all I see is the sick, bloated, old Pete.

The days run into each other and I don't realize how much he changes. Others do when they visit. His mother did not say anything about his decline.

I look at Pete's work folder, his evaluations. I can see why he was so respected. I always knew that if one of his employees didn't like him, that person wasn't a good worker.

SATURDAY, DECEMBER 15, 2001

Bad day for me. I am at loose ends, can't really do anything. Pete is bad, sleeping all day. I managed to get him to eat a little. Each time I got up last night, he was awake. The nurse says weeks, not months. I don't think we'll show him. His face is so bloated and he is bald on one side. I didn't realize how bad he looked until I found a picture of him about three years ago. I have to know that when he dies, only his body is left. I can't separate the two. I have a purpose now—taking care of Pete. What will my purpose be later? I don't think I can handle it. I told the nurse that everyone says I'm strong and I am not. She said I am stronger than I think. She said not many wives would do what I am doing. Most would get shift care in or send them to a nursing home. It made me feel good.

Ed Kenney is going down fast. The nurse sees him every day. He now has a catheter. No catheter for Pete. I will change him. Hospice nurse said the aide has commented on how much I do.

My mom went home Thursday. She will come back next Saturday. I think she feels good about being here.

SATURDAY, DECEMBER 22, 2001

Ed Kenney died last Sunday evening. I went to visitation with Matt and funeral by myself. It was hard, a preview of what is to come. It was a beautiful funeral. Henrietta is doing pretty well. I have not told Pete. Maitlens and Tadys stayed with Pete the times I had to be gone. Ed did not look like himself, even though his family thought so. It confirmed my belief that Pete should not be shown—only to family.

Have not heard from Morellis in over three weeks. I am so hurt by them and also by the Santamans. Jack is retired and can't find the time to spend with Pete. Jolene calls a couple times a week, usually from work.

The last time she was here, she said they would try to come more often; they haven't. Should I be feeling this hurt and disappointed? Am I being unfair? I can't believe they are doing this. They just seem to go on with their lives and can't make room for us. The last time the Santamans were here, I told them I didn't want anyone to feel guilty when this is over. Jolene said, "Well it will be their problem." I said, "I don't want to hear about it."

Karen and Frannie came out this afternoon bearing gifts. There was a big basket and a box full of gifts. Wow, did I make a haul. I am overwhelmed. I think they said Grace organized it. There was $230 in gift certificates and about twenty-five gifts.

Father said at Ed's funeral that when life throws you a curve, you pray for a miracle. When it doesn't come, you are confused. But maybe the miracle has already happened when you are able to accept what has happened. That is the miracle. I liked that. And it has been a miracle, with the help of Zoloft that I have done so well. No anxiety attacks. Those I couldn't handle. I need all the strength and courage God can give me to make it through the end. And then afterward—being alone.

I asked Tim Lavell to find someone to play the bagpipes at the cemetery. Everything has to be perfect.

SATURDAY, DECEMBER 22, 2001

Pete laughed today. My mom, Dick, and Cyndi came last night. I woke up to Dick reading the newspaper to Pete. Dick told Pete about smashing his finger the day before and Pete laughed. Mom stayed. Dick and Cyndi went home.

MONDAY, DECEMBER 24, 2001
CHRISTMAS EVE

Matt came for awhile. Matt was supposed to get Morgan at 7:00 p.m. tonight and take her back at 7:00 p.m. tomorrow night. Instead, he opted to let Tanya keep her until tomorrow morning so Matt can have her for Pete's funeral.

DECEMBER 25, 2001

Pete didn't even know it was Christmas. Matt came with Morgan. All of us seemed to be in a bad mood. The whole day was crappy, but we survived it. Thank you, God.

Sondra, Franklin, and Stacy came over. Sondra said she was sorry she hadn't been over. I said I just don't want anyone feeling guilty later. She said they and Santamans would come New Year's Eve.

I am so sad that Pete is so miserable. I hurt so much for him.

His mom called today—Merry Christmas and thanks for gifts—missed us. They were going to church. Dad wearing hat I had sent. How's Peter? Kind of crying at end.

SATURDAY, JANUARY 29, 2001

Kathy and Jim are supposed to come today. I asked Kathy to take my mom home. I told Mom she could come back in February. Will we still be doing this in February?

Yesterday, I bought a black coat and boots. Now if I could only lose about twenty pounds. I am so fat. I just continue to eat and don't exercise.

Haven't heard from Jolene since Monday when she called and my mom told her I was busy. They were so supportive in the beginning and now they have failed us—why? Jack has been retired for over a month and has not spent any time with Pete.

I pray a lot about the end. The end really scares me. I think my reaction will be violent. If there is time, I will have the boys here and I'll ask Maitlens and Brunsvolds to be here. They have been most supportive.

Woke up about 3:00 a.m. Could not get back to sleep. I do not like to take Xanax every night. Now I am exhausted.

The winter is here—that was one thing I didn't want to happen. Maybe God will grant us a few nice days when the time comes.

JANUARY 1, 2002

Not a great day. Pete slept most of the day. I was kind of down, didn't have a routine. Matt and Morgan were here. Last night, Santamans and Morellis came about 5:00 p.m. with snacks. Stayed until about seven-thirty. When they got ready to leave, Franklin hugged me and said, "I miss him." He broke down and cried. Franklin and Jack went outside. Sondra and Jolene stayed in with me. Jolene said, "We don't know what to do." I said, "Come over more." We'll see.

Today is Dad's birthday. I called and he sounded great.

Called Henrietta tonight. She sounded really good. I asked her what she thought Heaven was like. She said she never thought about it. Not me, I have to wonder, wonder, and wonder.

FRIDAY, JANUARY 4, 2002

Mark and Laura's anniversary. We kept Ian and Madison while they went out. Maitlens came with pizza.

SUNDAY, JANUARY 6, 2002

Have not left house since Friday noon. I'm having trouble. How long is this going to go on? Pete has had a couple of pretty good days. He has said a few words and has been awake a lot. I wonder what he's thinking when I cry. The ground is frozen now. I think we are all wearing down. Pete, me, and the boys. It has been eighteen months since this all started. Sometimes I don't like me. Sometimes I don't feel like I'm showing Pete enough affection, if only he would touch me. God, I know you are there and taking care of us, but I don't understand. Maybe I'm expecting too much.

Sometimes, I think the last eighteen months have been just a blur. Will I ever be normal again? Will I ever be able to work again? Will I be able to carry on without Pete? Should I go for counseling?

FRIDAY, JANUARY 11, 2002

Talked with Jolene on phone. Told her how I felt disappointed and let down by them and Morellis.

She tried to defend their busy lives, etc. There is no defense. When Pete started hospice, Jolene told me that she and Jack and Morellis would come out every night to help me get Pete to bed. Even though Jolene called me, I did not see her again for three weeks. When she came after three weeks, I reminded her that she told me they would come out every evening to help me. Jolene kind of punched me in the arm and said, "I've got a life, you know."

Tonight, Maitlens, Kris, DeBackers, Matt, and Morgan were here. Geri brought spaghetti pie for all.

SUNDAY, JANUARY 13, 2002

Took Morgan to get picture taken. Kids here, had lasagna. Saw Santamans coming out of Walmart. Talked a few seconds. I'm not sure if Jolene told Jack about our conversation. Maybe not. He would hold it against me and she wouldn't want that.

MONDAY, JANUARY 14, 2002

Kathy and Jim came for a few hours this morning. Pete slept most of the time. The weather today was miserable: cold, windy, and gloomy. Please give us nice weather. Pete sleeps a lot during the day, but I'm not sure how much at night. When I check on him, he is awake a lot.

Sometimes, when I read my notes, I think I am a mean, ugly person. I feel I am no longer a person. I don't exist. The other day, Pete responded to me and it was like, I'm real, I still exist. It is so unfair for a person like Pete to go through this. He hasn't been out of bed for six weeks. I don't think he knows what is happening to him anymore. I look at him and he just looks at me with questions in his eyes. Sometimes I just lose it; it hurts so much to see him this way. My feelings are so confusing. I don't want him to go on this way, but I don't want him to leave me. I think I'm ready for him to go and then he gets a little worse and I panic that he's going to die. Everyone says how strong I am. I don't see how I can make it through the end. The nurse says I'm doing good. She says not many wives could do what I'm doing. I'm glad I've stayed with Pete. I'm glad I'm able to take care of him.

Jesus, how long are we going to do this? How am I going to react if it happens during the night? I say I want it that way, so he doesn't have to struggle at the end. I told someone I might as well quit fussing about the end, because it's going to happen when and the way God wants it to. God is in charge.

God, could you help me lose weight? I'm a fat pig. I need to be healthy for Pete and I want to look good for the end. I guess that sounds terrible, but I want us to be perfect for Pete. It would make him proud.

FRIDAY, JANUARY 25, 2002

Wednesday, Mark and I went to the funeral home to make arrangements. We did okay; not as hard as I thought. I think I was totally spooked about picking out a casket. Mark and I put thought into what we picked out. Today, Ann and Millie sat with Pete while I went to look for a computer table. It was nice to be out. I was gone about three hours.

SUNDAY, JANUARY 27, 2002 6:30 A.M.

I am tired of all this. My arms hurt all the time. My right hip hurts, don't know what started that. I have a sore in my nose. I probably should go to the doctor. Every day blends into the next. Pete has been in hospice almost five months. I don't know what to say here. Everything I think of sounds like I'm whining.

Matt and his friend went and got my computer desk and end table, small drop leaf table, and two chairs and a child's rocker. I think Monday night I'll have the Tadys and the Brunsvolds over for dinner and Tom and Joel can get the desk in the room. We can unpack the computer and get it in place. I want to get online. I need to correspond with people. I would like to do some work.

I need to bathe Pete really good today and lotion him down. He was laying on his hand yesterday and now has this huge blood blister. The decadron causes his skin to be so thin. I don't think he is supposed to be on this much decadron for so long. I need to talk with Pete's radiologist. I will as soon as I get online.

When I got up this morning and walked in the kitchen, I couldn't hear Pete breathing. I stood there and watched and couldn't see him breathing. I wondered if this was the day. He moved his head ever so slightly. He was awake. Each morning, I greet him with cheer in my voice. "Hi, Stinker. How are you today?"

Sister Charlotte wonders why he keeps going. She says, "He looks at you with such love in his eyes." She said maybe he doesn't know he has permission to go. I told her I had talked to him and assured him he could leave me. The next day, I talked to him again about going to Heaven. I named all the people he would see, including Ed Kenney. I told him he should go when he was ready, not to wait for me. I would be okay. I said, "Are you ready to go to Heaven?" He said "Sure." He did not understand what I was talking about.

His mom called Tuesday night when I was at Brunsvolds. She called again last night. She was happy I had been out. She said I needed to get out. I said I wouldn't leave Pete with just anyone; I would stay home first. She said Dad was not doing well; half the time he doesn't know what's going on.

I need to clean the garage good. I don't know how to get the cobwebs. I guess a ladder. I would like to get some pegboard up so I can hang stuff, but I'm not sure where to put it. When I get rid of the reindeer and angel, I can put the tractor downstairs. I should clean the basement. The computer desk has a file drawer. I should be able to do bills at that desk and keep a few files there. I need to get organized.

I look at his picture and know he was a completely different person; so full of life and fun. I miss him coming in and saying, "My dahlin, I'm home." I miss his tender little good-bye kiss in the morning. I miss hearing him walk over to me to give me that kiss. I just miss his tender touch on my face. He would just lightly run his fingers over my face. I can do it and it feels like Pete. I miss the communication. I still try, but I have kind of gotten used to it. I miss not being taken care of. I miss all the special gifts. I missed no Christmas present. I'll miss Valentine's Day. Pete would be so upset if he could understand and know he hadn't gotten me gifts. His mind can accept so little. Sometimes I get a little spontaneous response, but usually nothing. He just looks at me with that question in his eyes.

The Santamans made their duty visit this week. Geri called Friday and Saturday.

WEDNESDAY, JANUARY 30, 2002

Monday evening, Tadys and Brunsvolds came over. Joe and Tom got my computer desk in the bedroom and the computer unboxed. A little rough doing it, but got it done. I fixed dinner—sausage spaghetti pie—a success. They stayed until almost 9:00 p.m. laughing and talking. Pete, sometimes almost smiled. He puckered his lips for a kiss from Nancy. When Tom leaned down, he puckered his lips; he will kiss everyone.

I am waiting for someone to hook up my computer and printer. I am anxious now. The desk is so efficient. I can take care of everything at that desk. I am anxious to get on email. I want to talk with Pete's radiologist. I could correspond with people at work. I would like that.

Talked with Judi last night. I asked her to be honorary pall bearer. She cried. I will also call and ask Mary. Mary has been very good to both of us. She took care of Pete, covered for him when we didn't know what was wrong with him. Judi and Mary both worked for Pete for many years.

This is really starting to wear on me and yet I don't want it to end. What will I do without Pete? I think of how mean I was to him when we didn't know what was wrong and I feel so guilty. He couldn't help it, but we didn't know that. I thought he should be able to fix himself. I never thought of a brain tumor. What was wrong with me?

MONDAY, FEBRUARY 4, 2002

Okay, God, I know we aren't supposed to make bargains with you, but please don't let Pete suffer. Please let him go to sleep and not wake up. Please, please don't let him suffer. He has suffered enough. Help me not to be bitter against those I think have failed us. What am I doing? I don't know what to do. I can't stand to watch Pete. He wants to eat, but it takes too much out of him. I'm not sure if it's because he can't breathe out of his nose or what. I feed him just a little at a time.

Mark stopped after work. He is having a hard time dealing with losing his dad. I can't help him. Together we just cry. I cry, he cries, he cries, I cry.

Sometimes I just can't accept what's happened. How could this happen to Pete?

SUNDAY, FEBRUARY 10, 2002

Pete was better by Wednesday. We put him on an antibiotic. Lots of coughing up phlegm. I think he and the babies had the same thing. He is still coughing, but doing 100 percent better. Thank you, God.

Franklin stopped Thursday. Walked over to Pete and Pete said, "Hi Franklin." Franklin was very pleased. Stayed about forty-five minutes. Sondra hasn't been here in over three weeks; Santamans over two weeks until they came on Friday on their way somewhere else. My talk did no good. I think they are selfish people who don't want this unpleasantness to be a part of their life. It is just too much for them to bother with.

Phil and Judy brought my mom Friday. She'll stay two weeks. She fusses over Pete and takes care of him. Kathy and Jim came Saturday and brought Mom and Dad. Pete's mom said she thought Pete was better. She had not seen him for two months. Kathy has a hard time every time she leaves.

I just went and lay in bed with Pete. I said, "Do you want me to lay down with you?" He says "Oh, sure." The other day, Mark and I were talking about Brad Hamil. I said he probably thinks I still owe him money. Pete pipes up and says, "Maybe not." Sometimes!

I can't tell you how wonderful our babies are. Both of them and yet so different. Morgan will kiss Grandpa, but no one else.

Working on a newsletter for school. New version of Publisher is great.

Making taco pie for dinner tonight.

SUNDAY, FEBRUARY 17, 2002

Hi God, how much longer? One day just rolls into another. My life is a blur and yet, how am I going to let go? Sometimes I dream he's okay. He can do things.

Over five weeks for Sondra. Teach me how to forgive. When this is over, Santamans and Morellis won't be my friends anymore. If they couldn't be here now, they certainly won't be here later.

My mom has been here the past week. She does help a lot. She does the laundry and keeps the kitchen cleaned up. She will feed Pete, give him drinks, and talk to him. Phil brought her up. Dick and Cyndi will come and get her.

Had Valentine's Day celebration. My last heart shaped meatloaf for Pete. Everyone here plus Kris and Shelby. Pete had been silent all day. Some days are like that. He is so sore between his legs. I got Desitin. Hope it clears up. No catheter!

MONDAY, FEBRUARY 18, 2002

Didn't see Santamans or Morellis. Jolene called Friday, said she would see us this weekend. Too busy for us. My life is going to change so much. I won't be included in so many things.

I feel so bad for Pete. And when I sit and watch TV or whatever, and don't pay attention to him, I feel guilty. Reminds me of Jesus and the disciples when they couldn't stay awake with Jesus.

Sometimes I am doing things and not spending the time with Pete. He slept most of the day, now he's awake.

Oh God, I don't think I can do this. I don't think I can lose Pete. He is my life. I don't know what to do. Please don't let him suffer.

SUNDAY, MARCH 3, 2002

Made it through January and February. Thinking maybe I won't need that black coat, and now it snows and nasty weather.

Pete slept from about 10:30 a.m. to 7:00 p.m. I changed him and tried to get him to eat. Just wanted to sleep. Does this mean the end is coming? God, I don't know what to ask for.

Thank you for my memories. They will get me through.

How could this happen to Pete? My Pete enjoyed life, such a good person. No chance to retire. Not fair. I'm bitter.

MONDAY MARCH 4, 2002

Bad day. He is weaker and not eating, only sleeping. This is what I was told would happen. I am losing it. Have cried buckets of tears. Snow all over the place. God, what do I want? I want to find him gone and then I think I want to be with him and hold him. I know you will decide what's best. Dreamed last night of anxiety attacks. I can do about anything except that. Thank you for Zoloft. All things are through you.

I still can't believe this is happening to Pete. My Pete is gone. The Pete who comes through the back door saying, "My dahlin, I'm home." I am so grateful for all my memories. He will never leave me; he'll never leave me, he'll always be with us. Give me strength to see this through.

Jolene is into e-mailing me. That's easy for her.

Figured out Santamans and Morellis. Gone on too long. Want to get on with life. Just a burden and bother they don't want. Rallied in beginning, but couldn't last it out. Youngs—I don't know.

SATURDAY, MARCH 9, 2002

The end is near. He hasn't eaten or drank anything for five days. He is in a coma state. No talking, not even opening his eyes. We wait and wait. The weather has turned bad.

Jolene is back. I don't know where she's been for six months.

The boys are here all the time. Dick and Cyndi were here Thursday and left Friday. Kathy and Jim came Saturday for a few hours. Pete's mom called and said she couldn't come because Dad was not doing well.

I fluctuate from good to bad. Some days I'm fine, others don't think I can do it. Mark is really struggling. I just need to remember that I can do all things through Christ who strengthens me.

Dick said when people ask him about Pete, he says sometimes a person will come into a family and makes a family better—Pete did that. Dick says that Pete made him a better person. What a wonderful tribute.

Maitlens coming home three weeks early. Don't know if they will get here on time. They will be home tomorrow. Barb and Joel in Phoenix. Were supposed to get home today, but she called and her mom is sick. Probably won't be back until Wednesday. Cutting it close. She and Nancy are in charge of after meal.

Matt staying with me.

SUNDAY, MARCH 10, 2002

Today could be the day. Pete has started really heavy breathing. It is so bad. I keep getting in bed with him and holding him. I think I will call Mark home from work so he can be here. Ron and Elaine came by today. Maitlens got home and they were here. Laura was here and sat by Pete for awhile. She cried. Both boys are going to spend the night here.

MONDAY, MARCH 11, 2002

Went to bed last night, Mark in the bedroom and Matt on the sofa. I kept getting up to check on Pete. Around 4:00 a.m. when I got up, his breathing was much slower. I woke both boys up. I got in bed with Pete so I was on one side and both boys sat beside him on the other. I sang over and over and over the Barney song, "I love you, you love me, we're a happy family, with a great big hug and kiss from me to you, won't you say you love me too." I sang that until Pete took his last breath. He was facing the boys, and they said he smiled before he took his last breath. It was 4:26 a.m. We just sat with him a few minutes. Then we cleaned him up, a bath and clean clothes, and we combed his hair. We tried to make him look spiffy. Then we started the calls. Sister Charlotte came, as did Gene, and Geri and Kris Maitlen. I got back into bed with Pete, while everyone else stood around him. They said the "Lord's Prayer." The hospice nurse came and called the funeral home. When they came, I would not let them zip up the bag when they put Pete into it. His face had to be free. The boys and I walked out to the hearse with him.

Pete Went Home

APRIL 12, 2002

Pete died on March 11, 2002 at 4:26 a.m. The boys and I were holding him. He smiled before he took his last breath. I didn't feel his soul leave his body.

Made it through the next few days with flying colors. Hope stayed with me. My mom came and stayed. Mom left on Good Friday. Hope on Easter Sunday. Went back to work on Monday. Had a good week. Weekend fine. Got sick on Monday and stayed home Tuesday and Wednesday. Back to work on Thursday— not feeling great. Left work—had two stops to make. Felt a lot of anxiety. Scared of anxiety attacks. Can do about anything but that. Have all along been afraid I'm going to crash. Definitely feeling less sure of myself. I'm starting to get scared about everything. I can do all things through Christ who strengthens me.

Where is my Pete? Bad dream, I'll wake up and he'll be here. I can't do this, Lord. I looked for Pete's prayer book. I thought he had two—couldn't find it. I wanted to say the rosary. I buried one prayer book with him.

Funeral

That was the last time I wrote in my journal. As I read it myself, I found that I did not write about the funeral. I need to do that. Pete's funeral was so perfect. It was a celebration! We were celebrating because Pete was in Heaven. Pete would have been so proud of our boys and me. We handled ourselves so well. Everything we did, we did for Pete.

• • •

Pete's funeral was so beautiful. I say that and it sounds really stupid, but it truly was. As I planned the funeral, I focused on what Pete would want and what would make him happy. Two of Pete's buddies and my brother gave tributes. They talked of what a great person Pete was, always there for everyone, always willing to be of service. They spoke of his honesty and his love of God. Funny stories were told. There was plenty of laughter in the midst of tears. The music was meaningful and beautiful. I picked three songs. One was an Irish song about a father dying and leaving his sons. The second one was titled "I'll Never Love This Way Again," that was from me to Pete. And then the final one, "Time to Say Good-Bye." Pete and I had first heard it in Las Vegas at the water display at Bellagio's. We stood and watched the water dance to the music and we both had tears running down our faces. After Pete got sick, he would listen to that song constantly. He told me he wanted it played at his funeral.

At the funeral, I had a friend read a letter that I had written to Pete several years ago. It was actually a college assignment that I never let anyone read before, not even Pete. The assignment was based on a scenario that terrorists had taken over a plane I was on. The terrorists told each passenger that they could write one good-bye letter because we would die the next day. Each student had to decide to whom to write the letter. I chose Pete. I remember sitting in the classroom writing it and getting so caught up in it emotionally as if it were really happening. I started to cry, so I excused myself and went for a walk. When I felt like I was in control again, I went back to the classroom and finished the letter. When I handed it in, I wrote a note to the teacher and asked her not to let anyone else read it as it was so personal. I never let anyone read that letter until the day of Pete's funeral and I let my friend read it to Pete. The letter was buried with him.

TRYING TO LIVE WITHOUT PETE

Pete had always been my protector. Always, always, whenever he thought something would bother or upset me, he would try to keep it from me. He took on so much himself so he could spare me. He never wanted me to worry or be upset about anything. I remember one day after he was gone, it came to me that I had to learn to rely on myself. I had no one to protect me any longer. That was scary.

• • •

After Pete was gone, I tried to take charge of my life. I had to. I didn't have Pete to do it for me. I created an e-mail address for Pete and I would write to him. I kept Pete's picture on my bed. I would make the bed in the morning and then prop the picture up in the middle. He still slept with me each night. Each night, I would climb into bed and the crying would begin. I would cry, I would scream, I wanted to die with Pete. I missed him so much. I missed taking care of him. But, I also knew I had to go on with life. I had two sons, and I had my precious grandchildren. God had taken Pete, but had given me two precious little girls. I knew they would never remember Pete themselves, but I would keep him alive for them, and they would truly know their grandpa. Well, it has worked. My girls talk about their Papa Pete all the time.

Pete is so much a part of their life. Many times, they ask me to tell them stories about Papa Pete. I once wrote a small book for them. Pete loved golfing, so the story was about Pete golfing with Jesus. Pete got a hole-in-one on a par five! After all, anything can happen in Heaven. I don't think more than a few days go by without one of the girls talking about Papa Pete.

• • •

I tried to create some kind of a social life for myself. I was no longer a couple and I was not invited to couple gatherings. I felt abandoned by some of the friends

I had been close to. It made me think that they had only liked Pete, not me. I joined a grief group, but only went once. My grief was still so fresh, I was very emotional, and didn't feel comfortable in the group.

On August 3, 2002, on Pete's first birthday after he died, I was having a particularly bad day. I got in the car and drove around. I found myself in a car lot looking at Miata's. I spoke with a salesman, got a price, and came home. The salesman called me and asked if I had made a decision. I told him I wasn't sure what I should do. At this point, I burst into tears and through my tears, tried to explain to him that my husband had died and today was his birthday. I had completely lost it. You can guess what that salesman was thinking. I drove that little Miata to church that evening. I still have it and do not plan to ever get rid of it. I always say I bought Pete a Miata for his birthday. I received criticism from a few people for making a frivolous purchase like that so soon after Pete died. Criticism would come at me from a lot of directions. I felt like I was doing okay with my decisions. I always thought about what Pete would want me to do and that was what I based my decisions on.

E-MAIL FROM PETER MANDER

One night, I went with some girlfriends to a seven-minute-date. That is where you move from table to table and talk to the opposite sex for seven minutes. I had such fun. I wasn't looking for a relationship, but I just needed to feel alive again. I e-mailed Pete and shared the evening with him. I laughed and I know he was laughing and shaking his head at me. I knew he was thinking, "I don't believe you did that, Donna."

Many nights, after going to bed, I would get up, get on the computer, and talk to Pete. It helped me greatly. In December, about nine months after Pete died, I wrote to him on a Sunday morning. I was particularly upset that morning and poured my heart out. It was a very personal e-mail. I ended it with asking Pete to send me a sign, not a maybe sign, but a for sure sign from him.

Later in the day, when I checked my e-mail, I had one from Peter Mander. I couldn't believe my eyes. What could this mean; how could this be? I opened the e-mail and found a message from someone who said apparently I had sent the e-mail to the wrong person. He said I sounded sad and he would like to help. I immediately wrote to him. It was like who are you and where are you? I found that his name was Peter Mander and he lived in England. We became friends though e-mail. What I discovered was that my Pete's email address was manderpeter and I had sent the email to petermander. I asked for a for sure sign from Pete, and boy did I get it. After I got that sign, I felt more at peace. I knew Pete was okay.

I received other signs from Pete: the TV coming on when I walked by, the cuckoo clock going off at the exact minute Pete died, lights suddenly coming on, pictures falling off the wall, and many more. One day, Mark, Erika, and I were outside weeding. We were up on a retaining wall when a big clod of dirt came up and hit Erika on the head. We looked down on the ground and no one was there. Mark said, "I just know Dad threw that dirt."

One of my favorite signs came on a day that I was having a particularly bad time. I went to the cemetery at noon. I stood at Pete's grave talking with him. I asked him to give me another for sure sign. I didn't want to guess it was a sign from him; I wanted to know for sure. I left the cemetery and while driving back to work, a huge buck deer very slowly strolled out on a fairly busy street right in front of me. I stopped my car and just watched that deer. I know Pete sent that deer to me. As Pete took care of me in life, he was still taking care of me in death.

I went to Sister Catherine for a while. She thought the e-mail account I set up for Pete was a wonderful idea. She felt it was very helpful for me. She did suggest that I write Pete a letter and then write a letter from Pete to me. It took me awhile to write the letter from Pete to me. I don't why it was hard, because I knew what Pete would say to me.

BLIND DATE

Weeks ran into months and the months ran into a year. One Sunday afternoon in March of 2003, my friend Geri called. She said that she and Gene had just gone to a retirement party for a friend. The friend's wife had died of breast cancer around the same time as Pete. Geri wondered if I would like to meet him. My answer was, "Sure, why not." Anyway, I received a phone call from a Chuck asking me if I would go to dinner with him. He lived at one end of the county and me on the other end, so we agreed to meet in the middle. Chuck told me he would be in a "candy-apple red van." We met in the parking lot of a Holiday Inn. We now laugh at the way that sounds.

Chuck took me to a very nice restaurant in another city. We found we had so much in common and lots to talk about. Chuck told me about the sickness and death of his wife, Bonnie. She died of breast cancer on December 14, 2001. I shared with him Pete's illness and death. After dinner, we went for a ride. The evening ended and Chuck asked if he could call me again. The answer was "yes." We started seeing each other about once a week.

Chuck and I had been seeing each other for several weeks, when at the end of one evening, as we were saying good-bye, I leaned over to him to kiss him on his cheek. I remember him pulling me to him and saying, "Give me a hug, I like being with you." After that evening, we were more comfortable with each other and started seeing each other more often. We spent a lot of time with our friends Geri and Gene.

• • •

Geri told me she was sure that she had a photo that had both me and Bonnie in it. I do not remember ever meeting Chuck and Bonnie, but since we were both friends of Geri and Gene's in the early days, it was very possible that we had been at the same social event. Geri found the picture, and yes, Bonnie and I were both in the picture. She also found a picture that had my two little boys and Chuck's little boy in it. Bonnie and I and our children had been at a birthday party for Geri's son.

Chuck and I discovered that we had many similarities in our former life. We were both married for over thirty-seven years, both our spouses died of cancer within three months of each other; we each had two children; Chuck and Pete both retired from the Rock Island Arsenal; we had lived only blocks from each other in the first years of our marriages; Chuck's and Pete's birthday is only four days apart; Chuck's son owned Pete's favorite golf course; of course, we had mutual friends in Geri and Gene; the list just kept getting longer.

A Proposal

Within a few months, Chuck told me he loved me. He said that he would like to get married. He had the whole thing planned in his mind. He told me that we could get married in my church, Geri and Gene could stand up for us, we could live in my house and he would get rid of his dog. I made one of the biggest mistakes of my life that night. I could have asked for anything and he would have agreed to it. I should have asked him to become a Green Bay Packer fan and I know he would have agreed. How did I not think of that? He now says he would not have agreed because he would never stop supporting the Chicago Bears. But I know better. That night he would have promised me anything.

OUR CHILDREN

My boys met Chuck and immediately liked him. I was surprised they accepted him so readily. It had only been a year since their dad died. The loss of their father was still so hard for them, but I have to believe that they saw some of the same qualities as their dad in Chuck.

Chuck had two children: a son and a daughter. I met Chuckie one night at a golf course. About a week later, Chuckie called and said that he and his wife Susie wanted to take us out to eat. We had a pleasant evening with Chuckie, Susie, and their son, Alec. Susie was and is a very warm person. She has the knack of talking with people and drawing them out. My boys love to talk with her. She listens and listens.

One Friday evening, when I was at a loss as to what to do, I decided to drive out to Chuck's and surprise him. When I arrived, there was another car in the driveway. I thought about driving away, but instead parked and went up to the door. Chuck answered the door and it was obvious that he was very happy and surprised that I was there. His company was his daughter and husband and three children. Well, I guess we were all surprised. Chuck went to take a shower, so I had some time to visit with Ann. Ann was pleasant and friendly, but I could feel some resistance. I guess, like my boys, her grief was still fresh. She was her daddy's little girl, and here, there was another woman in his life.

MARRIAGE FEARS

I was not sure I wanted to get married. I was confused. I had feelings for Chuck, but how could I when I still loved Pete? How can you love two men at the same time? I guess over time, I was able to work that out in my mind, but I did not want to get married. I had gained some independence and become stronger. I had learned to rely on myself instead of always having Pete to take care of my problems. I did not want to become weak again.

MEETING MY FAMILY

In July, my mom had surgery and was diagnosed with cancer. My siblings and I were all at the hospital because we were told that my mom was going to die. Chuck was with me the entire time; he never left my side. He met my mom and all my siblings. They all really liked him.

My brother, Dick, had been extremely close to Pete, but even Dick took to Chuck right away. Chuck had passed the test with all of my family.

Engagement and Marriage

Our children, Matt, Mark, Ann, and Chuckie had a chance to meet when Chuck's mother died. Even though it was a sad occasion, our kids got to spend a little time together. As I watched them talk, I could tell that there was some bonding going on.

In October, when Chuck and I were at a restaurant with Geri and Gene, Chuck presented me with an engagement ring and asked me to marry him. I knew he had the ring, he had had it for several months and had shown it to just about everyone; however, I did not know he was going to give it to me that night. I looked over at Geri and she had tears running down her face. You have to know Geri, she's a crier, like me.

. . .

We decided to get married in May, 2004. It was fun planning the wedding and reception. We knew we wanted a church wedding. There were so many people happy for us that we ended up inviting them all. We had a large church wedding with seven of our grandchildren being ring bearers and flower girls. When my boys started to walk me down the aisle, Madison yelled, "Daddy" and makes a bee line for her dad. Morgan saw this and ran to her dad. So down the aisle we came, me in the middle, with Mark and Madison on one side and Matt and Morgan on the other. I know Pete was watching us and he was smiling. I believe Pete sent Chuck to me.

Chuck and I had a picture of Pete and a picture of Bonnie on the altar. That was our way of having them at our wedding. We both knew that we would have their blessing.

Approval from Mom

Our married life was busy. Between the four children and many grandchildren, we were always on the go. My mom was still in the nursing home and we made monthly trips to see her. During the six and a half years mom was in the nursing home, she became very attached to Chuck. At one point, when we were leaving to go home, mom told Chuck she loved him, and then she said, "I never thought I would say that." I knew what she meant. She loved Pete like her own and never thought she could accept anyone else. Mom died January 24, 2009, one day after her ninetieth birthday.

UNITED FAMILY

Chuckie, Ann, Matt, and Mark have become brothers and sister. They really, truly, like each other and have a great time together. My boys, especially, are thrilled to have another brother and finally they have a sister. And, over the past six years, Ann's resistance is gone. I think that she realizes that Chuck and I love each other and are good for each other. And the bonus is, I now have a daughter!

In addition to Ian and Erika, Chuck and I have seven grandchildren, Alec, Kyle, Andrew, Morgan, Madison, Kelly, and Kara. We have a houseful when we all get together. The kids are cousins, not step-cousins. No one is allowed to use the word step!

GOD'S BLESSING FOR OUR MARRIAGE

Chuck and I feel very blessed that we have found each other. We have a good life together. Since we are both retired, we go south for the winter, coming home for the holidays and then returning to Florida. Around the end of March, we come home. We have similar interests. Together we go to movies, golf, ride bikes, do yard work, and work out at the gym. We try to stay active. And with our grandchildren, we are busy going to their activities. Through the church we attend, we realize we need to be better servants for God. We are active in our church, volunteering wherever there is a need. We find we are both more outspoken about our faith. We are members of a small group from church. The members of our small group have become close friends of ours. We love them and know we always have their support.

Our love for each other is special. We accept who we are and where we have been. Since we have both been through similar experiences with the death of our spouses, we accept and respect the feelings we still carry for Pete and Bonnie. Our love and feelings for them are with us always. They are still a great part of our lives.

Memories

My story started with a love between a man and a woman, for better, for worse, in sickness and in health. That love is still very much alive. It lives through my memories.

My memories are always with me, whether they are happy or sad memories. I believe that even when a person is no longer physically with us, memories allow them to remain alive. That is how I am able to live without Pete. He is with me every minute of every day. He will never leave me.

HAPPINESS JUST AROUND THE CORNER

At the beginning of my story, I said that sometimes happiness can be just around the corner. Just around my corner was Chuck. God blessed me with another wonderful man who became my husband. My life has been blessed! Through all the sorrow, fear, and grief, God was always with me. God never leaves us. His love is unconditional.

PICTURE SECTION

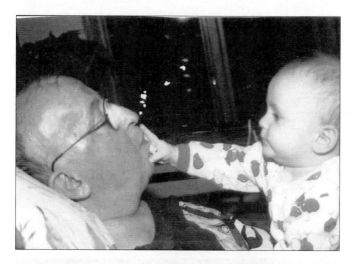

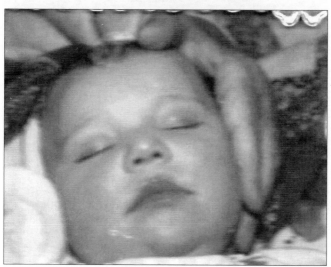

SUPPLEMENTS

*Child's book I wrote for Morgan and
Madison: Jesus and Papa Pete

*Three letters I wrote to Pete

*Letter I wrote from Pete to me

*July 2001 Update

*December 2001 Update

*March 2002 Update

*Photographs

Papa Pete and Jesus

This is a story about Jesus and a man named Pete.

Pete was grandpa to two little girls, Morgan and Madison. They called him Papa Pete.

Papa Pete was a good person. He loved his family and he loved Jesus.

One day Papa Pete got sick. He knew it wouldn't be too long before he would go to live with Jesus. Papa Pete started making plans. He knew in Heaven he could do all things he was never able to do before. He was so excited. He could hardly wait to go to Heaven. He knew Jesus would be the first one he would see.

On a nice Sunday afternoon, Papa Pete said good-bye to his family and he left them to go live with Jesus. When Papa Pete got to Heaven, Jesus said to him, "Pete, what took you so long, I have been waiting for you." Papa Pete told Jesus that even though he was excited to come to Heaven, it was very hard to leave Morgan and Madison.

Papa Pete told Jesus that he didn't want Morgan and Madison to miss him too much. Papa Pete said that he would never let them be lonely or sad, that he would always be in their hearts.

Then, Jesus and Papa Pete made plans. Papa Pete loved to golf, so that was the first thing he wanted to do. So, off he and Jesus went to golf. Papa Pete played better than he had ever played before. Papa Pete had always hoped he would get a hole-in-one. That is when you hit the ball one time and it goes right into the hole. So, guess what—Papa Pete got a hole-in-one. He was so excited; he was laughing and dancing with Jesus. Papa Pete sure was happy. He knew that all things were possible in Heaven, but he never dreamt he would get a hole-in-one. After that day, Jesus and Papa Pete played golf every day.

So, if you are ever on a golf course, look really, really hard, and you will see Papa Pete and Jesus. They will be all around you.

Written for Morgan and Madison Mander
January 2005

LETTER TO PETE (1)

Hi Honey,

It's 1:30 a.m. and here I am thinking about you. I do this nearly every night. I miss you so much. I have a CD on now to listen to the music you listened to every night. I'm hoping it will calm me and put me back to sleep.

I'm having a hard time writing this. I don't know why. There are so many thoughts I have. I think of you constantly. Sometimes I miss my old Pete and sometimes I miss my sick Pete. I miss taking care of you. I miss your little lips puckering up to kiss. You didn't lose that. I miss feeding you. But, I think I'm eating for both of us. I think I'm eating myself to death. I am so fat. I look terrible. Each day I think I'm going to stop all this eating and each day I pig out. I have no control. Could you help me with this? It's so unhealthy to be this way. I need to take better care of myself for the boys.

LETTER TO PETE (2)

Good Morning Sweetie,

You have been gone two months today. I am numb. I have your picture in bed with me so I can reach over and look at your sweet little face. I touch and stroke and kiss your face. It brings me great comfort. I feel you are here with me. I need to really, really know you are here—not just a maybe, but for sure. Remember we talked about it and you promised if there was a way, you would come back so I could feel your presence. I am waiting. As I think of it, I believe you sent me to the monastery. That thought just popped into my mind. I think it is a good choice. Sister Catherine told me to write this letter to you and then write one to me from you. Gosh, the things I could make you say.

Matt bought a Corvette. He said he learned a lesson from you. You waited your whole life for a new truck, finally got one, and only drove it a few months. You know how he will baby that car. He rarely takes it out of his garage. Mark has your truck. He is so proud to be driving your truck. I think I always know what you want me to do. I'm thinking about getting me a little sports car, but have mixed feelings on it. That one, I'm not entirely sure how you would feel. Let me know.

There is a beautiful little yellow bird on the deck now. The bucket of seed fell over and he is having a feast. Remember our nest of robins in the jade plant? That was fun to watch.

I'm doing pretty good, I think. And I think that is because you are still with me and helping me through this. I feel your presence. I just want to feel your touch.

The bedroom is my sanctuary. I have you with me.

Tell me, who did you see before you took your last breath. You smiled. What a gift that was to us. And thank you for waiting for us so we could hold you when you went home. We felt great peace.

You know how I have always been afraid of dead bodies. Your body did not scare me. We cleaned you and shaved you and got you all gussied up before we let anyone come.

You looked so handsome in your suit. I think it was a new one you hadn't worn.

I think of the person you were, such a lively person, and it's so hard for me to believe you are not going to walk in that back door. We had a great love, didn't we? Not many have what we did. It was so special. I am so grateful for all the years we had—for the life we had. I am not bitter. I know you wouldn't want me to be. I'm glad I'm not. I know God was in control the whole time, still is.

What do you do in Heaven? You know I've always wondered that. I wouldn't want you to just be floating around. I'm sure you have seen Ed. Are you two golfing and coaching? I wonder so much about Heaven.

I know you haven't left me completely. Help me to feel you for sure. I will always love you.

MLF Donna

LETTER TO PETE (3)

Hi Honey,

Still haven't written that letter from you to me. I reread what I wrote to you and I cry and cry. When I read it, it is all new; I don't even remember writing the particulars. I have no memory. I am numb. I am nothing without you. You took care of me and now I have no one. When you were sick and lying in that bed, I would look so deeply into your eyes so we would never lose that connection. I know we still have it. How am I going to live without you? I can't do it. I need you back. I have no one to touch in church. I have no one to put my cold feet on in bed. I have no one to love me. How can you be gone? Just a nightmare. Wake me up.

LETTER I WROTE
FROM PETE TO ME:

MAY 14, 2002

My Dahlin,

I am still with you. I would never leave you completely alone. When the time is right, you'll know I am with you.

Do you know how proud I am of you? You have done so much and have been so strong! But, I've always known how strong you are, you were the one who felt you were weak. No one could have done a better job than you.

I loved the time you spent with me while I was sick. And, oh, the breakfasts. Man did we eat! You took such good care of me. And you prayed with me every night. You kept saying, "Do you know how much I love you?" Yes, I know how much you love me. I never doubted it. We had something very special— few people have it.

You know I am with you in the bedroom. I know when you talk to me and I feel your kiss when you kiss my picture. You are doing fine, honey. Don't let anyone tell you that you aren't.

I feel bad that some of our friends have kind of abandoned you. If I were there, I would punch them for you.

You are taking care of being strong for the boys. I could never do as well as you are. I would be lost without you.

You know you have always wondered about Heaven. Well there is no way I can describe it, it is so beautiful. I am saving a special place for you. We will be together again. Until then, I want you to live your life to the fullest. Have fun, laugh; I am with you every time you laugh. There is laughter here in Heaven. How could there not be?

I have become acquainted with our Jeff. You were right. He met me and took me home. How wonderful it was that you and the boys were with me at the end. There could not be a more beautiful way to go home.

Remember honey, I love you, I love you, I love you, a thousand times I love you. TDMOEL

UPDATE ON PETE MANDER

(sent updates to approximately 100 people)

JULY 6, 2001

We would like to give everyone an update on Pete and encourage you to continue your prayers. We believe there is power in prayer and we must believe that Pete will be healed. I have felt recently, (maybe, just me being me), that I need to give everyone a nudge and keep the momentum going. We must never rest easy until the doctors say Pete is healed.

So, the purpose of this letter is to give you a progress report and also to ask that you aggressively continue to pray for us.

Pete had surgery for a malignant brain tumor on December thirteenth. The doctors were not very optimistic about his long term survival, but we had and have other plans. In my conversations with the doctors, I have told them we do not want to hear anything about life expectancy. I have told them we have a lot of hope and prayers and I don't want anyone taking that hope away from us. Since then, the doctors have treated us differently. They have become our friends. They have been aggressive in their treatment. Pete completed six weeks of five-days-a-week radiation. We then waited two months and went back for another MRI. The MRI showed that the tumor was smaller. The radiologist recommended that Pete have radial surgery—that is one massive dose of radiation to the center of the tumor. This is a fairly new procedure and a lot more complicated than regular radiation. Pete had this done about six weeks ago. We have another appointment July twenty-sixth. He will have another MRI to see if the latest radiation did any good. A common side effect to the radial surgery is an abscess on the brain. If this would happen, the surgeon has talked about a second surgery to remove the abscess and at the same time plant a chemo water in the tumor. Again, a fairly new procedure. With this procedure, Pete would not have to take the regular chemotherapy. This is a waiting game and it is very hard to wait.

Physically and mentally, Pete is not the same. He is slow in his movements and his short-term memory and thought process is not what it used to be. I think this is mostly from the radiation. I finally got the doctor to admit that radiation kills good cells as well as bad cells. The radiologist says that his memory will probably never be what it once was, but hopefully will get better. It is very hard for both of us. I pray for patience every day, and I don't always succeed. We spend a lot of time together, sometimes just being close. He likes for me to rub his head and I do. I tell him that I'm trying to make the hair grow back. When I think about the last seven months, I thank God that that we have had this time. It has been horrendous, but also has been wonderful, because we have had the time together. We talk about everything and try to plan for everything. We are there for each other. When I am low, he is brave for me, and when he is low, I am brave for him.

Our lives have not been the same since we received the diagnosis on December seventh, and we know that no matter what happens, our lives will never be the same. We are different! Pete and I pray together each evening. We started out just reciting prayers. We have grown from there. We also read Scripture on healing; it is surprising how many times God tell us He wants us to be well and be healed. He also tells us that we must fight, and boy do we fight. We are constantly kicking Satan to stay away from us. We have a list of people we pray for each evening. For ourselves, we do not pray for a healing because we have already claimed a healing. We do pray for strength, courage, patience, and the ability to accept whatever God brings our way. We ask that we will be good witnesses for others. We give thanks for our life and all we have. Are we brave all the time—the answer is no; we still have to deal with our fears.

We have with our friends claimed a healing for Pete. We had a prayer service where we anointed him with oil, and many times blessed him with holy water. We have listened to the advice of others who know how we should fight this disease, and we are doing it all.

Just when I am having a bad day, someone walks into my life and helps. At work, I have met several ministers. As soon as I find out they are ministers, they are mine. I ask them to pray for us. They have been wonderful. I practically run people down on the street to ask them to pray. I never miss a chance to ask people to pray for us. I have no pride when it comes to asking for prayers. We have churches and religions from all over this country praying for us. We feel so good when we hear that someone or some church is praying for us. We have received tremendous prayers and support from family and friends. The number of cards that Pete received was overwhelming. He still receives cards occasionally. And, almost always people also ask about me. It gives us a real lift to know that people care and are continuing to pray. We plan to win this battle and we need all of you to aggressively continue your efforts. Let us hear from you.

Pete just heard that his retirement has come through, so he will be retiring within the next two months. We are happy about this and at the same time we will have to deal with what he will do with his time. He is not driving now, so he is somewhat house-bound. If you have any thoughts, let us know.

God bless all of you for your continued support and prayers.

During all of this, we have had two very special blessings, two new granddaughters—Morgan born December seventh, the day we received the diagnosis, and Madison was born July fourth. Our sons are always available for us. We keep in touch nearly every day. They make life a lot easier for us. We are truly blessed with our family.

P.S. Please pass this letter on to anyone and everyone who will pray for us!

Pete Mander Update

You have all been so much a part of our life this last year, I want to share with you the latest news on Pete.

In late July we went to Iowa City for a check-up and MRI. We received good news. The radiologist said the tumor was "stable if not smaller." From that day on, Pete became progressively worse. Since we were told the tumor was stable, I felt it must be radiation damage, necrosis caused from radiation or maybe even a stroke. I talked with the radiologist and we increased the steroid to reduce the swelling on the brain. That did not help. By early September, Pete was totally incapacitated. We went back to Iowa City for another MRI. At that time, the radiologist said that what he saw on the MRI was "consistent with tumor growth." He did not feel it was radiation damage, etc. He indicated we had a couple of choices. We could be aggressive and have another surgery to remove part of the tumor, which might give Pete a few extra months, or we could take him home, make him as comfortable as possible, and wait. The radiologist said Pete could live a few days, a few weeks, or even a couple of months, but he really thought it would be soon because of Pete's condition. Our son Mark, my brother Dick, and my sister-in-law Cyndi were with me. Together, we decided we didn't want to put Pete through another surgery. It was time to let go and let God.

Following the second MRI, Pete improved considerably. He started talking, he could feed himself, and could understand some things. Within the last few weeks, he has regressed again. He hardly speaks at all; he just lays and stares. Occasionally, he says something and I know he understands for that moment. Pete always knows who I am and he is not in any pain. I have been fortunate to have my sister, my brother's wife, and my mom come and stay for a few weeks at a time to help me. They took care of me while I took care of Pete, and on days that I went to work, they took care of Pete. Pathway Hospice also has been a wonderful source of assistance and guidance. We have friends who come and stay with Pete some days while I go to work in the mornings. Pete and I spend a lot of time together. He has always taken care of me and been my strength, and now I am taking care of him and I am his strength. Pete will not be going to a nursing home or a hospital. He is staying in his home with his family.

Before this happened to us, I thought that if someone were going to die, it would be best to have a heart attack and be gone quickly rather than go through a long illness. I was wrong. I would not trade the last twelve months for anything. I would like to say it has prepared us for what's coming, but it has not in many ways. I will never be prepared for a life without Pete. What has happened is a coming together of our family. Pete and I and the boys have always been a close family, but this has strengthened that closeness. I am so proud of our sons; they have dug deep and gone beyond anything I thought they were capable of. They are so free with their feelings for their dad in the way they talk to him and touch him. They are taking care of him just the way he took care of them. The boys have amazed me. I have amazed myself. We are doing things I never thought we could and most of the time with good humor. We try to make Pete laugh and see the humor in the situation. Most of time it works.

And so we wait. Each day is a gift from God. There are days when I question why this has happened to Pete rather than someone else. I voice this to Pete and he says, "That's the way God wants it." I realize how lucky we have been to have thirty-seven years of marriage, two great sons, and four precious grandchildren. Pete is such a good grandpa.

We sit the babies on his lap and he kisses them and strokes them. He has joy for the moment. I am most concerned and sad about Ian (five years). He and Grandpa were great pals before Pete got sick. Ian was crazy about his grandpa and Pete felt the same way. They did lots of yard work together. Ian was glued to Grandpa and helped him with everything. For Ian, it was Grandpa, Grandpa, and Grandpa. Since Pete has been sick, Ian has pulled away from him. Ian is smart and is preparing for what he knows is going to happen. He said to me one day, "Grandpa is getting ready to go to Heaven."

And there is no doubt where Pete is going. I have talked to him about it. I told him that he was so lucky because he was going home to be with God. I told him that he would be met by Jeff, our first son. I told him that it was his job to go to Heaven and be with Jeff and my job was to stay here with Matt and Mark until I join him later. Pete is not afraid; he just isn't ready to leave yet. I have told him when he is ready to go, I want him to go, and I don't want him to stay for us.

One day as I was bathing Pete, I cried and told him how sad I was that he was so miserable. He looked up at me and said, "You are miserable, too." Another time, as I was dressing him, he said to me, "It takes a lot of love to do this." The other night, as my friend and I were trying to move Pete from the chair to the bed, we were discussing who should stand where to get the job done. Pete was very silent and just put up with us. We got him in the wheelchair (kind of) and over to the bed where we again discussed how we were going to get him into bed. Out of nowhere, Pete said, "Somehow, I don't have much confidence in this." He then smiled. So, we have our happy moments, too.

I will never be able to adequately tell all of you how much it has meant to Pete and me to know we have your prayers. You are our support system. I feel we have all shared this together. Even though I have questions, I know God is in control and is taking care of our family. We do not know when the end will come, but I know that I am going to need tons of strength to get through it. Please continue to keep our family in your prayer.

Have a blessed holiday season and give thanks to God for all you have.

Final Update

GOOD-BYE TO PETE

MARCH 2002

Pete died Monday, March 11, 2002, at 4:26 a.m.

I have boxes of thank you notes to all of you who have been our source of strength for the last year and a half. Instead of thank you notes, I want to thank you by sharing with you the last few months of Pete's life, and some of my favorite memories of him.

When the weather was nice in September and October, I would find a way to get him in the car and take him for drives. We always went to B-Bops and got a burger and fries. We would sit in the parking lot and eat. Then when Krispie Kreme opened, we first went to B-Bops and then Krispie Kreme. He ate everything and so did I. It was the one thing we could do together.

By November, he was weaker, but we were still able to get him up every day. On Thanksgiving Day, Matt and I got him in the wheelchair and took him to the neighbor's. He sat in the garage with the guys and smoked a cigar.

It was hard for me to see the deterioration in him because one day ran into the next. For a while, I worked half days when my family and friends would come and stay with Pete. But one day I woke up and he looked so terribly, terribly sick. I knew I wouldn't leave him again. He was mine to take care of. He needed me and

I needed to be with him. If I did leave him for a few hours, sometimes I would come home and find him distraught. All I had to do was climb in bed with him, talk soothingly, and he would start to relax.

On a Sunday in early December, I bathed Pete, washed his hair, put cologne on him, and got him all gussied up because we were having company. Our friends came and sang joyful and uplifting songs. Sometimes we overuse the word fellowship, but fellowship is what we had that day. We felt renewed and even a little hopeful. That was the last day Pete got out of bed.

Our Hospice Aide came five days a week to give Pete a bath. On the weekends I did this. I really did it up good. He was mine, he was captive, and I cleaned and trimmed and shaved and oiled and vaselined and cologned until he was shining. I enjoyed doing this. I wanted him to look good and feel good. I would always tell him how handsome he looked when I was done. The aide would not shave up close under his nose because Pete didn't like it. When I shaved him, believe me, he got a close shave.

As the days sped along, he got weaker, talked less, and was less responsive. We knew the end was near. I talked to Pete many times about going to Heaven. I told him to save a place for me because I would be joining him before he knew it. I spent time in bed with him talking to him, touching him, and just being next to him.

He stopped eating and drinking on Monday, March fourth. We were told this would be the progression of his illness. Pete did not eat or drink the whole week. On the following Sunday, his breathing became very labored. I called Mark home from work. Matt was already home having stayed overnight with me for a few nights. Both boys stayed overnight. I kept checking on Pete; it was important to me that we were with him at the end. Around 4:00 a.m., as I sat by his bed listening to him, his breathing paused for just a second. I woke both boys up. I climbed in bed with Pete and held him and the boys sat on the other side and held him. I talked to him and I sang to him. Within minutes, he stopped breathing. I looked at Mark and he gave me a nod to say it's over, and then Pete smiled and took one last breath. I did not see the smile, the boys did. I looked over at our sons and said, "We did it. We kept Dad at home like he would have wanted." The three of us felt at peace. As Pete took care of us in life, he took care of us at the end by leaving us with a smile. It was his last gift to us.

I got up after a few minutes. I told the boys I wanted to bathe their dad before anyone saw him. We bathed Pete, shaved him, put clean clothes on him, oiled him, cologned him, and put fresh sheets on the bed. Then we made our phone calls. As a few friends and Sister Charlotte arrived, we formed a circle around Pete's bed and prayed. When the men from the funeral home came, Matt, Mark, and I stayed with Pete until he was in the hearse.

How did we do all this? We had God in our midst! That is the only answer. And He stayed with us through the next several days while we had visitation and the funeral. I had spent many hours planning the visitation and funeral because everything had to be just right for Pete. Right after the last visit to Iowa City, when we knew there was nothing more that could be done, I said to the boys, "We have to do everything right, we have to make Dad proud." Everything we did, every plan we made, was for Pete.

We went to visit the cemetery the day after we buried Pete. I was surprised at my lack of emotion and voiced this. Mark said, "Mom, you have been grieving for a year and a half."

My reply was, "Dad has been gone for a long time. I know he isn't here."

Before Pete was sick, he and I had many conversations about dying. I made him promise that if he died first, if there was any way possible for him to come back and let me feel his presence, he would. I know he is still with me. Pete would never leave me completely. He would want me to be happy and he would want me to laugh and keep telling funny stories about us.

There was a long line at visitation. Many, many people came to say good-bye to Pete. We had a lifetime of pictures displayed. The funeral was beautiful, full of love and laughter and raw emotion. Our sons looked so handsome. Everything was right. Pete would have been so proud.

Pete will live with me forever. My memories of him will carry me through life. Our sons and I will keep him alive for our grandchildren.

MY FAVORITE MEMORIES

- Pete and Ian planting the garden and doing yard work.

- Pete and Ian standing together in the back yard and peeing in the bushes.

- Pete and Ian and Erika making popcorn.

- Pete holding and kissing our baby girls. How Grandpa loved them.

- Morgan feeding Grandpa animal crackers and Madison napping on Grandpa with his hand cradling her head.

- No matter how old they got, when the boys left our house, Pete always said, "Be careful."

- Pete sitting on the front porch of our first home, holding our six-month-old boys, one in each arm.

- Pete ate cereal each morning. He would wake me up with the click, click of the spoon against the bowl. I brought this to his attention. He started using a plastic spoon.

- Pete's gentle, gentle, almost-not-there kiss he would give me each morning before he left for work.

- Waking up in the morning with Pete running his hand so softly over my face. Such a sweet, gentle touch. That was love!

- Pete coming in the back door after work singing out, "My dahlin, I'm home."

- Telling funny stories about himself (The diarrhea one was the best).

- Pete's lips puckering up to kiss each and every person who leaned down to him during the last couple of months.

- The smell of Old Spice and the sight of his wing tips.

Whatever your kindness or gift was to us—cards, visits, flowers, memorials, food, prayers, smiles—no matter how small or how big, I thank you from the bottom of my heart.

Let me hear from you. And if you have a favorite memory of Pete, I would like to hear it.

INDEX

PETE AND DONNA'S IMMEDIATE FAMILY

Matthew and Mark, sons; Laura, daughter-in-law; Tanya, Morgan's mom; Morgan, Madison, and Erika, granddaughters; Ian, grandson

DONNA'S FAMILY

Mom; Hope and Ruthie, sisters; Philip and Johnny, deceased brothers; Dick, brother; Cyndi, sister-in-law; Judy, Phil's friend

PETE'S FAMILY

Mom and Dad; SueAnn and Kathy, sisters; Bill and Rick, brothers; Jim, brother-in-law; Aunt Patsy

FRIENDS

Barb and Joel Brunsvold; Elaine and Ron Foht; Mike and Diane Kavanagh; Henrietta and Ed Kenney; Karen and Tim Lavell; Gene and Geri Maitlen; Judy McKinley; Sondra and Franklin Morelli; Ann Mulvey; Jolene and Jack Santaman; Nancy and Tom Tady; Candi; Don; Frannie; Grace; Karen; Kris; Millie; Shelby; Youngs

MISCELLANEOUS

Father Tommy; Sister Charlotte; Sister Catherine; Pam, deceased friend

CHUCK'S FAMILY

Ann, daughter; Chuckie, son; Greg, son-in-law; Susie, daughter-in-law; grandchildren, Alec, Kyle, Andrew, Kelly, and Kara